THE
INTERACTION
OF LAW
AND RELIGION

THE
INTERACTION
OF LAW
AND RELIGION

HAROLD J. BERMAN

SCM PRESS LTD
Bloomsbury Street London

334 00700 3

First British edition 1974
published by SCM Press Ltd
56 Bloomsbury Street, London

© Abingdon Press 1974

Type set in the United States of America
Printed and bound in Great Britain by
REDWOOD BURN LIMITED
Trowbridge and Esher

● To Eugen Rosenstock-Huessy (1888-1973)

● Preface

This book comprises the Lowell Lectures on Theology delivered at Boston University in 1971. The lectures are printed substantially as they were spoken, together with a short introduction, a postscript, and some annotations.

The lectures were addressed to a general audience—they are not theological in the conventional sense of that word—and I hope that in their printed form they will be of interest to all persons who wish to understand the relationships between the institutional structures of a society and its fundamental beliefs.

My thanks are due to Dean Walter Muelder and Professor Robert Nelson of the Boston University School of Theology and to Dean Paul Siskind of the Boston University School of Law, who were responsible for extending to me the invitation to give the lectures. Also I wish to thank the panel of commentators—George Avery, Walter Miller, William Stringfellow, Bascomb

7

Tally, and Joseph C. Weber—who, at the close of the final lecture, discussed some of the questions I had raised. Their comments have helped me to prepare the postscript and the footnotes. In addition, I am grateful to William Alexander and William Anderson, who were then law students at Harvard Law School, for valuable assistance in research during the summer of 1970 when the lectures were beginning to take shape; I am also grateful to James Gordley, then a graduate law student, who made some important comments on the manuscript. Finally, I am indebted to my colleague Roberto M. Unger of the Harvard Law School and to Edward Long of the Department of Religion of Oberlin College, with both of whom I discussed the lectures at length and who both gave me the very great benefit of their criticisms.

H. J. B.

Cambridge, Massachusetts
May 29, 1973

Contents

 Contents

Introduction

This is a book of lectures, not a treatise or monograph. It is meant to affirm and to challenge, not to demonstrate by elaborate proofs. Although it deals with eternal questions, the book claims to be timely rather than timeless.

The principal affirmation is that law and religion are two different but interrelated aspects, two dimensions of social experience—in all societies, but especially in Western society, and still more especially in American society today. Despite the tensions between them, one cannot flourish without the other. Law without (what I call) religion degenerates into a mechanical legalism. Religion without (what I call) law loses its social effectiveness.

Some listeners were concerned that more emphasis was not placed on the conflicts between law and religion. There is, indeed, a danger of oversimplifying their reconciliation by failing to see that it is a dialectical

11

synthesis, a synthesis of opposites. The postscript has been written partly to allay that danger. But for reasons stated there as well as in the lectures themselves, I am convinced that we have heard too much about the separation of law and religion and not enough about their fundamental unity. I should perhaps emphasize that I am speaking of law and religion in the broadest sense— of law as the structures and processes of allocation of rights and duties in a society and of religion as society's intuitions of and commitments to the ultimate meaning and purpose of life.

When prevailing concepts of law and of religion become too narrow, and hence the links between the two dimensions are broken, a society becomes demoralized. The existing institutional structures and processes lose their sanctity, and conversely, the sacred values upon which the society is founded are viewed as mere hypocrisy. Eventually such demoralization may yield to widespread demands for radical change. This was the situation confronting America (and not only America) when these lectures were given. For several years radical movements had been agitating this country and others: the youth culture, the New Left, the peace movement, women's liberation, black militants, and others. Also the larger ideologies of democracy, socialism, and various forms of communism, which had seemed almost inert in the 1950s and early 1960s, underwent a revival in the late 1960s. All these movements attacked existing institutional structures and processes in the name of various

basic values—I would call them religious values—upon which Western civilization is founded. Most of them, however, offered no viable alternative institutional structures and processes with which to replace the existing ones, and some of them were altogether antilegal and antistructural. They were therefore at the mercy of the "Establishment," which to a considerable extent responded by simply reasserting "law and order."

In 1973, as this introduction is being written, most of the radical movements of 1968-1972 seem to have subsided, at least temporarily. We seem to have reverted to a vague demoralization. Perhaps the lectures are more timely than ever. What they say to the Establishment is that a people cannot live for long without engagement, without enthusiasm, without struggle, without faith. What they say to the Radicals is that a revolution cannot succeed if it lacks a great vision of institutional and structural change, a vision of law, and not merely a vision of faith—a vision, in fact, of the interaction of law and faith. But where the whole society has such a vision, revolution is not necessary; it has already happened.

The four chapters that follow represent four different perspectives. The first is anthropological: it deals with law and religion as dimensions of all cultures and argues that in all cultures, including our own today, law and religion share certain elements, namely, ritual, tradition, authority, and universality. These religious elements of law are not often stressed by contemporary legal scholars. Instead, law is generally presented as a secular, rational,

utilitarian system—a way of getting things done. But as soon as one goes behind the law in books to the processes by which it is made, interpreted, and applied, one sees the symbols of the sanctity which infuses it. That is as true of an American legislature or court as it is of any tribal procedure. Law has to be believed in, or it will not work. It involves not only man's reason and will, but his emotions, his intuitions and commitments, and his faith.

The second chapter represents a historical perspective. It deals with the influence of religion on Western law during the past two thousand years, including the influence not only of traditional Judaism and Christianity but also of the secular religions of democracy and socialism into which Christian attitudes and values have been translated during the past two centuries. The main theme is that our basic legal concepts and institutions derive much of their meaning from a historical development in which religion has played a major part. Indeed, the very concept of the ongoingness of law, of its organic growth over generations and centuries, is itself a religious concept rooted in Judaism and Christianity. Moreover, in Western history since the eleventh century the ongoing legal tradition has been interrupted periodically by great revolutions, each of which has attacked the pre-existing system of law in the name of a religious or quasi-religious vision and each of which has eventually created new legal institutions based on that vision.

The third chapter shifts attention from the religious

dimensions of law to the legal dimensions of religion. Here the perspective is philosophical. An effort is made to expose the fallacies of those schools of religious thought which pose irreconcilable contradictions between law and love, law and faith, or law and grace. In all religions, even the most mystical, there is a concern for social order and social justice, a concern for law, both within the religious community itself and in the larger social community of which the religious community is a part. In both Judaism and Christianity law is understood to be a dimension of God's love, faith, and grace; both Judaism and Christianity teach that God is gracious *and* just, that he is a merciful judge, a loving legislator, and that these two aspects of his nature are not in contradiction with each other. Antinomian tendencies in current Protestant and Catholic thought—the belief that structures and processes of social ordering are alien to man's highest qualitities and aspirations—have a counterpart in the secular apocalypticism of the "counter culture" as expressed in many of the communes that sprang up in America in the 1960s and early 1970s. Yet the spontaneity, joy, self-discovery, togetherness, and other great qualities and aspirations of such groups cannot be realized over a long period of time without structures and processes, without norms.

The perspective of the fourth chapter is harder to classify. It explores the predicament faced by Western man in a revolutionary era—such as the present era from which we are only beginning to emerge—when the exist-

ing legal and religious systems have broken down and there seems to be nothing available to replace them. This might be called an eschatological perspective. Living between two worlds, we experience the dying of the old orders of law and religion and anticipate their regeneration. What is dying is not so much their institutional structure (which indeed seems to have a remarkable staying power) as the foundations on which the structure is built. An important part of those foundations is the presupposition that law and religion are wholly separate aspects of life—that the way we run our society need have nothing to do with our deepest intuitions and our deepest commitments, and vice-versa. Behind this radical separation of law and religion is a dualistic mode of thought that has recurrently threatened the integrity of Western man during the past nine centuries. Subject is radically separated from object, person from act, spirit from matter, emotion from intellect, ideology from power, the individual from society. The overcoming of these dualisms is the key to the future. The new era which we anticipate is one of synthesis. The dying of the old dualisms calls for rebirth through the kinds of community experiences—on all levels, from communes to the United Nations—that reconcile legal and religious values.

Having recapitulated the main themes of the chapters, I am struck by the discrepancy between the small size of this book and the magnitude of those themes. To treat them systematically and comprehensively would require

something like Dr. Eliot's five-foot shelf. This, on the other hand, is intended to be a germinal book. Yet even from the point of view of conventional scholarship, it may serve as a useful prospectus for future research.

In fact, its main themes have not been the subject of extensive treatment in scholarly literature. There is no work of anthropology, so far as I know, which deals directly with the role of ritual, tradition, authority, and universality in legal processes, although there are books which deal with those four elements in the great religions of the world. There is also no work of historical scholarship, so far as I know, which deals directly with the influence of religion on the historical development of Western law; indeed, there seems to be no extensive study even of the influence of the canon law of the Roman Catholic Church on the secular legal systems of the West, although the fact that it had a very considerable influence on them can hardly be denied. And the few studies of the influence of Puritanism on English and American law in the seventeeth and eighteenth centuries only begin to tell the story. Moreover, the historical derivation of Western concepts of democracy and socialism from Western concepts of Christianity, though often hinted at, has not to my knowledge been the subject of systematic research.

On the main subject of the third chapter—antilegal tendencies in Christian thought—much has been written; the chapter summarizes the literature and cites some of it in the annotations. However, on the second theme of the

chapter—antilegal tendencies in the counter culture and in the communes—much empirical research remains to be done.

Finally, the fourth chapter opens up the question of the differences in attitudes toward law between Eastern and Western Christianity as well as between Christian and non-Christian religions. It also opens up the question of the relation between the sociology of revolution and Christian eschatology. Again, these are subjects that have often been suggested—sometimes in ways quite similar to the ways that they are suggested here—but not systematically studied and elaborated.

And so the expansion of the book is left to the reader. If he will use it as a starting point for further research, the author need not worry about either its brevity or its eclectic character. (Indeed, any study which attempts to integrate established scholarly disciplines will appear incomplete and eclectic to specialists in any of the disciplines.)

Yet this book is not offered primarily as a work of scholarship in the usual sense of that much abused word. It is offered primarily as a self-reminder and as a reminder to others that the compartments into which we have divided the world are not self-contained units, and that if they are not opened up to each other they will imprison and stifle us. The lawyers study and practice their concepts and techniques; the seminarians concern themselves with things of the spirit; the professors profess their various disciplines. But the gods of law and the

gods of religion and the various other gods of our society will not be able to give us the vision we need to keep our integrity as a people and as a civilization. That vision must transcend the divisions which now threaten to destroy us. I speak here not primarily of divisions of nations and races and classes and sexes and generations, but primarily of divisions within our minds and hearts, divisions in the way we see and feel things. What we have seen and felt hitherto as divisions must be understood now as interacting, interdependent dimensions of a single historical process.

I.

⬤ Religious Dimensions
of Law

Western man is undergoing an integrity crisis—the kind
of crisis that many individual men and women experience in their early fifties when they ask themselves with
utmost seriousness, and often in panic, what their lives
have stood for and where they are headed. Now we are
asking that question not only as individuals but as nations and as groups within the nations. Our whole culture
seems to be facing the possibility of a kind of nervous
breakdown.[1]

One major symptom of this threatened breakdown is
the massive loss of confidence in law—not only on the
part of law-consumers but also on the part of law-makers
and law-distributors. A second major symptom is the
massive loss of confidence in religion—again, not only on
the part of those who (at least at funerals and weddings)
sit in the pews of our churches and synagogues, but also
on the part of those who occupy the pulpits.

21

Historians will tell us that in every generation the complaint is made that people are losing their religious faith and their respect for law. And it may also be true that there are more churchgoing, law-abiding Europeans and Americans today than there were in previous periods of our history. Yet the symptoms of an integrity crisis are unmistakable. Among the earliest signs were those given after the first World War by artists and poets and novelists—men like Picasso and Joyce—whose work revealed that traditional conceptions of space and time and even of language itself were disintegrating, cracking up. Then came the intellectual upheavals of the 1930s when social scientists told us that the traditional social, political, and economic structures had lost their validity. Europe was torn by new revolutionary mythologies, while America withdrew into herself. Ironically, the Second World War gave the nations of the West a temporary lift; we found that we were, after all, capable of collective action and of personal sacrifice for traditional common goals. This spirit was artificially maintained for a time after the war, especially by the campaign against communism. But since the late 1950s we have increasingly experienced a sense of futility and a premonition of doom, the most visible signs of which are the progressive demoralization of the cities, the deep frustration of a significant portion of the youth, and the incapacity of the nations to act decisively in the interests of peace either at home or abroad.

What makes this an integrity crisis rather than some

other kind of crisis is precisely its relation to the loss of confidence in religion and in law. In the centuries prior to World War I religion and law—especially in America—were the patrimony of our collective life. They embodied our sense of common purpose and our sense of social order and social justice—"the style of integrity" (in Erikson's words) "developed by [our] . . . civilization." [2] Our disillusionment with formal religion and with formal law is thus symptomatic of a deeper loss of confidence in fundamental religious and legal values, a decline of belief in and commitment to any kind of transcendent reality that gives life meaning, and a decline of belief in and commitment to any structures and processes that provide social order and social justice. Torn by doubt concerning the reality of those values that sustained us in the past, we come face to face with the prospect of death itself.

How are we to explain our disillusionment with law and with religion? There are, of course, many causes. One of them, I believe, is the too radical separation of one from the other. That in turn is partly the result of our failure to make the right connections between formal legal and religious systems, on the one hand, and the underlying legal and religious values to which I have referred, on the other. Both the law schools and the schools of theology bear their share of responsibility for the narrowness and the rigidity of our thought on these matters.

If we see law in dictionary terms merely as a structure

or "body" of rules laid down by political authorities, and similarly see religion merely as a system of beliefs and practices relating to the supernatural, the two seem connected with each other only very distantly or in only a few rather narrow and specific respects. But in reality both are much more than that. *Law is not only a body of rules; it is people legislating, adjudicating, administering, negotiating—it is a living process of allocating rights and duties and thereby resolving conflicts and creating channels of cooperation. Religion is not only a set of doctrines and exercises; it is people manifesting a collective concern for the ultimate meaning and purpose of life—it is a shared intuition of and commitment to transcendent values.* Law helps to give society the structure, the gestalt, it needs to maintain inner cohesion; law fights against anarchy. Religion helps to give society the faith it needs to face the future; religion fights against decadence.[3]

These are two dimensions of social relations—as well as of human nature—which are in tension with each other: law through its stability limits the future; religion through its sense of the holy challenges all existing social structures. Yet each is also a dimension of the other. A society's beliefs in an ultimate transcendent purpose will certainly be manifested in its processes of social ordering, and its processes of social ordering will likewise be manifested in its sense of an ultimate purpose. Indeed, in some societies (ancient Israel, for example) the law, the Torah, *is* the religion. But even in those societies which make

a sharp distinction between law and religion, the two need each other—law to give religion its social dimension and religion to give law its spirit and direction as well as the sanctity it needs to command respect. Where they are divorced from each other, law tends to degenerate into legalism and religion into religiosity.

In this first chapter I shall speak chiefly about the dependence of law upon religion.

Anthropological studies confirm that in all cultures law shares with religion four elements: ritual, tradition, authority, and universality.[4] In every society these four elements, as I shall try to show, symbolize man's effort to reach out to a truth beyond himself. They thus connect the legal order of any given society to that society's beliefs in an ultimate, transcendent reality. At the same time, these four elements give sanctity to legal values and thereby reinforce people's legal emotions: the sense of rights and duties, the claim to an impartial hearing, the aversion to inconsistency in the application of rules, the desire for equality of treatment, the very feeling of fidelity to law and its correlative, the abhorrence of illegality. Such emotions, which are an indispensable foundation of every legal order, cannot obtain sufficient nourishment from a purely utilitarian ethic. They require the sustenance of a belief in their inherent and ultimate rightness. The prevailing concept in contemporary Western societies that law is primarily an instrument for effectuating the policies of those who are in control is, in the long run, self-defeating. By thinking of law solely

25

in terms of its efficiency, we rob it of that very efficiency. By failing to give enough attention to its religious dimensions, we deprive it of its capacity to do justice and possibly even its capacity to survive.

The Secular-Rational Model

A heavy burden of proof rests on one who asserts that not only in past eras of our own history and not only in nonwestern cultures but also in modern, technologically advanced countries of the West, including the United States today, religious elements play an indispensable part in the effective working of the law.

The conventional wisdom is the opposite: that although law in most cultures may have originally been derived from religion and although during certain eras such as the Catholic Middle Ages or the age of Puritanism our own law may have contained religious elements, these have been gradually purged away during the past two centuries so that today there is almost nothing left of them; and further, that modern law is to be explained solely in instrumental terms, that is, as a consciously elaborated means of accomplishing specific political, economic, and social policies.

Contemporary social science characterizes modern law by the words "secular" and "rational."[5] The alleged secularism of law is linked with the decline of the belief in either a divine law or a divinely inspired natural law. The law of the modern state, it is said, is not a reflection of any sense of ultimate meaning and purpose in life;

26

instead, its tasks are finite, material, impersonal—to get things done, to make people act in certain ways.

This concept of the secular character of law is closely linked with the concept of its rationality, in the special sense in which that word has come to be used by social scientists. The lawmaker, in inducing people to act in certain ways, appeals to their capacity to calculate the consequences of their conduct, to measure their own and others' interests, to value rewards and punishments. Thus legal man, like his brother economic man, is conceived as one who uses his head and suppresses his dreams, his convictions, his passions, his concern with ultimate purposes. At the same time, the legal system as a whole, like the economic system, is seen as a huge, complex machine—a bureaucracy (in Max Weber's definition)—in which individual units perform specific roles according to specific incentives and instructions, independently of the purposes of the whole enterprise.

The contrast between this conception of law and the conception of religion that goes with it has recently been expressed by Professor Thomas Franck of New York University. Law, he writes, in contrast to religion "has . . . become undisguisedly a pragmatic human process. It is made by men, and it lays no claim to divine origin or eternal validity." This leads Professor Franck to the view that a judge, in reaching a decision, is not propounding a truth but is rather experimenting in the solution of a problem, and if his decision is reversed by a higher court or if it is subsequently overruled, that

27

does not mean it was wrong but only that it was, or became in the course of time, unsatisfactory. Having broken away from religion, Franck states, law is now characterized by "existential relativism." Indeed, it is now generally recognized "that no judicial decision is ever 'final,' that the law both follows the event (is not eternal or certain) and is made by man (is not divine or True)." [6]

On the other hand, Franck recognizes that to proclaim this philosophy too loudly may involve a certain cost in popular respect for legality. The legal system is apt to become "more open to challenge and less likely to inspire unquestioning mass loyalty." We would go one step further and ask what it is that inspires not unquestioning mass loyalty to law but simply a general willingness to obey it at all. If law is merely an experiment, and if judicial decisions are only hunches, why should individuals or groups of people observe those legal rules or commands that do not conform to their interests?

The answer usually given by adherents of the instrumental theory is that people generally observe the law because they fear the coercive sanctions which will otherwise be imposed by the law-enforcing authority. This answer has never been satisfactory. As psychological studies have now demonstrated, far more important than coercion in securing obedience to rules are such factors as trust, fairness, credibility, and affiliation.[7] It is precisely when law is trusted and therefore does not require coercive sanctions that it is efficient; one who

rules by law is not compelled to be present everywhere with his police force. Today this point has been proved in a negative way by the fact that in our cities that branch of law in which the sanctions are most severe—namely, the criminal law—has been powerless to create fear where it has failed to create respect by other means. Today everyone knows that no amount of force which the police are capable of exerting can stop urban crime. In the last analysis, what deters crime is the tradition of being law-abiding, and this in turn depends upon a deeply or passionately held conviction that law is not only an instrument of secular policy but also part of the ultimate purpose and meaning of life.

Law itself, in all societies, encourages the belief in its own sanctity. It puts forward its claim to obedience in ways that appeal not only to the material, impersonal, finite, rational interests of the people who are asked to observe it but also to their faith in a truth, a justice, that transcends social utility—in ways, that is, that do not fit the image of secularism and instrumentalism presented by the prevailing theory. Even Joseph Stalin had to reintroduce into Soviet law elements which would make his people believe in its inherent rightness—emotional elements, sacred elements; for otherwise the persuasiveness of Soviet law would have totally vanished, and even Stalin could not rule solely by threat of force. Though he unleashed all his terror against potential enemies, he invoked "socialist legality" as a source of support among the rank and file of the people, and in the name of

"socialist legality" and "stability of laws" he attempted to restore the dignity of the Soviet courts and the sacredness of the duties and rights of Soviet citizens.[8]

Similarly, the idea that law is wholly existential, wholly relative to circumstances of time and place, that it cannot be measured by standards of truth or of rightness but only by standards of workability, that it "lays no claim to divine origin or eternal validity," [9] is also self-defeating. It is tenable in the classroom but not in the courtroom or in the legislature. Judicial decisions or statutes that purport to be merely hunches or experiments lack the credibility upon which observance of law ultimately depends—observance not only by "the masses" but by all of us, and especially by judges and lawmakers.

Once in 1947 when the late Thurman Arnold, who as a teacher and writer carried the theory called "legal realism" to the point of genuine cynicism, was urging upon a class at Yale Law School his view that judges decide solely according to their prejudices, a student interrupted to ask whether when Arnold himself was on the bench he did the same. Arnold paused before answering; one had the impression that he was transforming himself from Mr. Hyde to Dr. Jekyll as the professor in him yielded to the judge. He replied, "Well, we can sit here in the classroom and dissect the conduct of judges, but when you put on those black robes and you sit on a raised platform, and you are addressed as 'Your Honor,' you *have* to believe that you are acting according to some objective standard." [10]

Common Elements of Law and Religion

The secular-rational model neglects the importance of certain elements of law which transcend rationality, and especially of those elements which law shares with religion. This neglect is connected with the fallacy of viewing law primarily as a body of rules and of underestimating the context in which rules are enunciated. Once law is understood as an active, living human process, then it is seen to involve—just as religion involves—man's whole being, including his dreams, his passions, his ultimate concerns.

The principal ways in which law channels and communicates transrational values are fourfold: first, through *ritual*, that is, ceremonial procedures which symbolize the objectivity of law; second, through *tradition*, that is, language and practices handed down from the past which symbolize the ongoingness of law; third, through *authority*, that is, the reliance upon written or spoken sources of law which are considered to be decisive in themselves and which symbolize the binding power of law; and fourth, through *universality*, that is, the claim to embody universally valid concepts or insights which symbolize the law's connection with an all-embracing truth. These four elements—ritual, tradition, authority, and universality—are present in all legal systems, just as they are present in all religions. They provide the context in which in every society (though in some, of course, to a lesser extent than in others) legal rules are enunciated and from which they derive their legitimacy.

31

THE INTERACTION OF LAW AND RELIGION

It is striking that Thurman Arnold, in the episode which I have related, stressed the effect upon himself, as a judge, of the symbols of office—the robes, the furniture of the courtroom, the rhetoric of respect. Such symbols are supposed to impress not only the judge, but also all other participants in the proceeding, and indeed the society as a whole, with the fact that one charged with the dread responsibility of adjudication should put aside his personal idiosyncrasies and personal prejudices, his *pre*judgments. Similarly, the jurors, the lawyers, the parties, the witnesses, and all others involved in a trial, are given their respective roles by the ceremonious opening ("Oyez! Oyez!" with all rising), the strict order of appearance, the oaths, the forms of address, and the dozens of other rituals that mark the play. This is no free-for-all in which everyone "is himself." On the contrary, each participant subjects his own personality to the requirements of the legal process. Thus the great ideals of legal justice are dramatized: objectivity, impartiality, consistency, equality, fairness. As the English say, justice must not only be done, it must also be *seen* to be done. This does not mean that unless it is seen it will not be accepted; it means that unless it is seen it is not justice. In Marshall McLuhan's famous phrase, "the medium is the message."

The rituals of law (including those of legislation, administration, and negotiation, as well as of adjudication) like the rituals of religion are a solemn dramatization of deeply felt values. In both law and religion the

dramatization is needed not only to reflect those values, not only to make manifest the intellectual belief that they are values that are useful to society, but also to induce an emotional belief *in* them as a part of the ultimate meaning of life. More than that, the values have no existence, no meaning, outside the process of their dramatization. By virtue of their symbolization in judicial, legislative, and other rituals, the ideals of legal justice come into being not primarily as matters of utility but rather as matters of sanctity, not primarily as ideals but rather as shared emotions: a common sense of rights, a common sense of duties, a demand for a fair hearing, an aversion to inconsistency, a passion for equality of treatment, an abhorrence of illegality, and a commitment to legality.

Moral philosophers attribute beliefs concerning justice to man's capacity to reason, but we are speaking here of something different, namely, man's emotions; and we are speaking not of his moral emotions but more specifically of his legal emotions.[11] Justice Holmes once wrote that even a dog knows the difference between being stumbled over and being kicked. We would add that even a dog becomes upset if his master rewards him one minute and punishes him the next for the same thing. The rituals of law symbolize (bring into being) the fundamental postulate of all legal systems, even the most rudimentary, that like cases should be decided alike: they raise that postulate from a matter of intellectual perception and moral duty to a matter of collective faith.

33

It is no overstatement, therefore, to speak of fidelity or faithfulness to law. This is essentially the same kind of dramatic response to the sacred, to the ultimate purpose of life, that is characteristic of religious faith. Law, like religion, originates in celebration and loses its vitality when it ceases to celebrate.[12]

Law also shares with religion its emphasis on tradition and authority. All legal systems claim that their validity rests in part on continuity with the past, and all preserve such continuity in legal language and legal practices. In Western legal systems, as in Western religions, the historical sense of ongoingness is comparatively very strong, so that even drastic changes are often consciously explained as necessary to preserve and carry forward concepts and principles handed down from the past. But in other cultures as well, the drive for consistency leads to some sense of continuity with the past. The Moslem khadi has a reputation to preserve and will not judge differently each time. Even the Greek oracles were supposed to reflect a hidden consistency. The law need not be eternal, but it also must not be arbitrary, and therefore it must change by reinterpreting what has been done before. The traditional aspect of law, its sense of ongoingness, cannot be explained in purely secular and rational terms, since it embodies man's concept of time, which itself it bound up with the transrational and with religion.[13]

Similarly, the law need not be revealed in the sense of written by God on tablets of stone (indeed, there are

few such reported cases); yet the law is invariably appealed to, when parties are in dispute, as though someone in authority once embodied it in a constitution or statute or precedent or custom or learned book or some other authoritative source. In most political, economic, or social experience of a nonlegal nature (say, an election campaign or an industrial program or a family crisis or a neighborhood feud), people feel free to propose new courses of action based solely on utility; but if a legal question is posed, alternative solutions are almost invariably debated in terms of rules and decisions laid down by those in authority. Of course, the power to interpret the rules and decisions is also the power to remake them. Nevertheless, we say that the court is "bound" by the statute; the legislature is "bound" by the Constitution; even the framers of the Constitution felt themselves to be "bound" by a "higher law." They made it, but they did not make it out of whole cloth.

Except in cultures where law and religion are not differentiated, the specific rituals, traditions, and authorities of the law are not generally the same as the rituals, traditions, and authorities of religion, although they may overlap to some extent. Nor are the emotional responses which they induce the same, although they, too, may overlap. The legal emotions differ from the ecstasy or sense of grace or anxiety or fear of damnation that Søren Kierkegaard and Rudolf Otto attributed to the "idea of the holy." [14] Nevertheless, legal emotions share with religious emotions the same sense of "givenness,"

35

the same reverence, the same urgency. In secular religions the givenness, the sanctity, may be attached to the state rather than to God, or to the court, or to the party, or to the people.

Also there is the same potentiality for abuse of ritual, tradition, and authority in law as in religion. Here the chief danger is that symbols needed to reflect and induce commitment to higher values may become objects of reverence for their own sake, ends in themselves, rather than "outward and visible signs of an inward invisible grace." In religion this is called magic and idolatry. In law it is called procedural formalism—as in trial by ordeal or by battle or by ritual oaths. The whole history of Western law from the twelfth century on has been marked by efforts, by no means always successful, to break away from the domination of such formalism.[15] The secularists and the rationalists would have us escape from magic and idolatry and formalism by entirely rejecting emotional commitment to legal values, together with the ritual, tradition, and authority which reflect and induce them. They would rely wholly on an intellectual commitment to law as a useful instrument of policy in promoting the finite, material interests of individuals and groups in society and would disparage efforts to ground logic and policy in an emotional commitment to law as an integral part of the ultimate meaning of life, with the "penumbra of mystery" (as Reinhold Niebuhr has put it) which "surrounds every realm of meaning."[16] What I am urging is that law will not survive such a

desiccation, such a draining of its emotional vitality. On the contrary, law and religion stand or fall together; and if we wish law to stand, we shall have to give new life to the essentially religious commitments that give it its ritual, its tradition, and its authority—just as we shall have to give new life to the social, and hence the legal, dimension of religious faith.

The fourth major commitment which law shares with religion is the belief in the universality of the concepts and insights which it embodies. Such a belief should be distinguished from the theory of natural law, which may be wholly independent of religion. Indeed, a secular and rational theory of natural law is not only entirely possible but is the most widespread form which current natural-law theory takes. The morality inherent in law itself, the principles of justice which are implicit in the very concept of adherence to general rules, may be perceived by moral philosophers without reference to religious values or religious insights.[17] Also, anthropologists are able to show by empirical observation that no society tolerates indiscriminate lying, stealing, or violence within the in-group, and indeed, the last six of the Ten Commandments, which require respect for parents and prohibit killing, adultery, stealing, perjury, and fraud, have some counterpart in every known culture. In fact many natural-law theorists consider a religious explanation of law to be superstitious and dangerous. Such theorists are able to demonstrate by reason and observation alone that basic legal values and principles cor-

respond to human nature and to the requirements of a social order. Contracts should be kept; injuries should be compensated; one who represents another should act in good faith; punishment should not be disproportionate to the crime. These and a host of other principles reflect what reason tells us is morally right and what in virtually all societies is proclaimed to be legally binding.

It was the Greeks who taught us this kind of thinking. It was they who first translated religion into philosophy. Since Plato we have not needed the gods to tell us what virtue is; we can discover it by using our minds. So, at least, we have said, although as Christopher Dawson has shown, the Greek secularization of philosophy also involved a deification of reason. Today we are no longer so convinced that thought can be as "pure" as the philosophers have assumed.[18] We have learned that when the mind tries to operate wholly independently, when it pretends to stand wholly outside the reality it observes, it breaks down and becomes skeptical even of itself.

On a more pragmatic level, the trouble with a purely intellectual or philosophical analysis of morality is that the very inquiry, by its exclusive rationality, tends to frustrate the realization of the virtues it proclaims. The intellect is satisfied, but the emotions, without which decisive actions cannot be taken, are deliberately put aside. Therefore all legal systems require not only that we recognize the proclaimed legal virtues with our intellect but also that we become committed to them with our whole being. And so it is by a religious emotion,

a leap of faith, that we attach to the ideals and principles of law the dimension of universality. To say, for example, that it is against human nature to tolerate indiscriminate stealing and that every society condemns and punishes certain kinds of taking of another's property is not the same thing as to say that there is an all-embracing moral reality, a purpose in the universe, which stealing offends. And when a society loses its capacity to say *that*—when it rests its law of property and of crime solely on its rational perception of human nature and of social necessity and not also on its religious commitment to universal values—then it is in grave danger of losing the capacity to protect property and to condemn and punish stealing.

The Revitalization of Law

But is there not a serious danger that an emphasis on the law's commitment to universal truths will serve to deify existing social structures and thus to bring us to idolatry by another route? Must not the prophetic aspect of religion and the tension between law and love, law and faith, law and grace, be preserved for the sake of the integrity of religion, whatever may be the consequences for law? And are not the consequences for law, too, apt to be disastrous if law is not only respected but also sanctified?

These are questions to which I shall return in subsequent chapters. However, there is one aspect of them that has to be dealt with immediately, or everything said thus far will be misunderstood. It is *not* to be

supposed that since law is failing to communicate its values to large numbers of people in the urban ghettos, in the new youth culture, in the peace movement, and elsewhere, therefore we should set about simply to manipulate its rituals, traditions, and concepts of authority and universality, leaving the underlying social, economic, and political structure unchanged. It is *not* suggested that the way to overcome our integrity crisis is to prop up the legitimacy of the old legal system with various religious devices plus a return to the Puritan ethic.

On the contrary, a recognition of the dialectical interdependence of law and religion leads us in the opposite direction—in the direction of fundamental social, economic, and political change and of new legal solutions for the acute problems confronting us: unemployment, racial conflict, crime, pollution, corruption, international conflict, war. But in order to find new *legal* solutions to such problems we must give new vitality to law—for law as it now presents itself, shorn of its mystique and its authority and its role in the grand design of the universe, is too weak a reed to support the demands we place upon it. In many areas of American life law reform will not work because law will not work—until it finds rituals that effectively communicate its objectivity, until it recovers its sense of ongoingness and of binding power, until it rediscovers its relationship to universal truths concerning the purpose of life itself.

Let me give a few practical examples. The breakdown in administration of criminal law is perhaps the most

striking. Our press as well as our scholarly literature has been full of accounts of the grotesque and humiliating character of our system of detention prior to trial, our system of disposition of cases by negotiation between the prosecutor and the accused, and our prison system. We seem to be reliving the times of Charles Dickens. There is no easy way out of this morass; nevertheless, an understanding of the religious dimensions of law can show the direction to be taken. We need new forms of investigation, new forms of hearing, and new forms of custody which will dramatize humaneness and sympathy in the treatment of offenders, on the one hand, and, on the other hand, indignation both at their offenses and at the conditions which produce the offenses. It is not enough to remove the usual criminal sanctions of imprisonment or fines for so-called "crimes without victims" (drunkenness, drug abuse, prostitution, gambling, homosexuality), thereby releasing a very large amount of the time and energy of the police, the courts, and the detention agencies. This is advocated by the experts, and to a considerable extent it should be done; but it is only half the solution. The other half is to devise new legal procedures both inside and outside the criminal courts—new liturgies, if you will—for dealing with cases of persons who engage in such conduct (to the extent that it is antisocial), including new ways of enlisting the participation of the community—of psychiatrists, social workers, and clergy, and also of family, friends, neighbors, and fellow workers—before, during,

41

and after the case is heard. To speak of "decriminaliza-tion" of the law, as some do, is misleading. To speak of offenders as "ill persons," as some do, is also misleading. We must find ways of hearing such cases and treating such persons humanely and creatively while at the same time expressing society's condemnation, not of them as persons, but of their conduct and of the conditions under-lying their conduct. This, indeed, is in our religious tradition; and it makes sense.[19]

Another example is that of political crimes. We need new forms of proceedings, new rituals, for dealing with cases like those in recent times of the Chicago Seven where the defendants seek to use the courtroom as a platform for proclaiming their political views.[20] One clue to what is possible in such cases was provided in the case of the Catonsville Nine, an anti-war group ac-cused of burning some hundreds of draft cards. The judge permitted the trial to be conducted in a relatively informal way. The defendants, who included the priests Daniel and Philip Berrigan, had ample opportunity to express their motives, with which the judge and the prosecuting attorney were sympathetic. Yet the illegal actions were condemned.[21] Thus the trial served a larger purpose than putting guilty persons in prison. All trials should be educational, not vindictive. It is better to delay the proceedings than to bind or gag or ridicule a de-fendant. It is better that he go free than that the court —to paraphrase Holmes—should do an ignoble thing. A trial should provide a catharsis, not a new assault upon

our dignity. It should dramatize, not caricature, the values implicit in the legal process.

We also need new forms of procedure in many types of civil cases. New types of family courts are needed to deal with problems of family disorganization. In the area of automobile accidents, nonjudicial agencies should determine the amount of damages, thus avoiding the travesty of leaving it to a jury to determine the extent of the plaintiff's losses, including his pain and suffering; but at the same time new procedures should also be devised in automobile cases to expose and condemn negligent driving as well as defects in our automobile technology. Once again, the law should not settle for convenience only; it should insist on educating the legal emotions of all who are involved—the parties, the spectators, the public.

Apart from the adjudicative process, we need new forms of proceedings in local and state government in order to revitalize branches of law relating to public education, pollution, welfare, low-cost housing, fair employment practices, and other like matters. Here the community itself can begin to create the new quality of life that many of our youth have rightly demanded. But new forms, new rituals, are needed to channel popular participation in creative rather than destructive ways. One important reform that has been undertaken in many places is the establishment of the office of Complaint Commissioner (the so-called Ombudsman), who will effectively investigate and act on citizens' complaints. A

43

second, more general suggestion is to establish procedures for encouraging the expression of popular sentiment—"town meeting" types of procedures—without permitting domination by too vocal minorities.

Ultimately, broader participation of the public in the processes of the law is an important key to its revitalization. People must feel that it is *their* law, or they will not respect it. But they will only have that feeling when the law, through its rituals and traditions and through its authority and its universality, touches and evokes their sense of the whole of life, their sense of ultimate purpose, their sense of the sacred. At the end of the First World War, Max Weber charged that "the fate of our times is characterized by rationalization and intellectualization and, above all, by the 'disenchantment of the world.'" [22] It is true that many branches of our law have suffered from such a disenchantment, though often without benefit of much rationalization or intellectualization. But despite all our disillusionment, it is wrong to suppose that America is without faith. The faith of America is expressed above all in participation itself, in the sense of people in local communities and groups, all over the country, acting somehow together. This is the heritage of Puritan congregationalism, on the one hand, and of the social and religious experience of ethnic immigrant communities on the other. It would be tragic if America's tradition of participation were allowed to die. Even in the raw, ugly context of the modern city, we have a chance to bring back into public life

"the ultimate and most sublime values" which Weber said had "retreated" either into mystical experience or into intimate personal relations,[23] by enlisting people of all kinds, and in large numbers, in the processes of law enforcement, in new types of parajudicial proceedings, in local and state administration, and in many other areas of public life.

We have considered religion and law in the broadest possible terms—religion as man's sense of the holy, law as man's sense of the just—recognizing that in all societies, though in widely varying ways, law draws on the sense of the holy partly in order to commit people emotionally to the sense of the just. This is true among the Barotse tribesmen of Africa, where witchcraft stands behind legal custom and mediation as a kind of last resort. It was true in another way in traditional China, where law was seen as a necessary evil but was nevertheless dialectically related to Confucian gentility and politeness as well as to neo-Confucian ancestor worship and emperor worship. The interdependence of the sense of the holy and the sense of the just is true also of Soviet Russia, where the law proclaims that socialist property is sacred and where socialist eschatology—the coming of a communist utopia—is an important factor in the development of legal institutions and of legal doctrine. It is true of the United States, where not only traditional Christianity and Judaism but also the secular religion of the American way of life give sanctity to

45

basic legal norms and procedures; indeed, in few other legal systems does one find such explicit reliance on divine guidance and divine sanctions and so great a reverence for constitutional appeals to universal standards of justice.[24]

By emphasizing the interaction of law and religion we may come to see them not just as two somewhat related social institutions, but as two dialectically inter-dependent dimensions—perhaps *the* two major dimensions—of the social life of man.

Taken alone, so broad a concept may obscure the tensions that exist between law and religion in given historical situations. That is, of course, the danger of an anthropological approach—that it tends to view culture as an integrated, harmonious whole. Some anthropologists writing on religion treat virtually everything in the culture they are writing about as religion; and similarly, some anthropologists writing on law treat virtually everything in the culture they are writing about as law.

Despite this danger, I believe we must start with an anthropological perspective on law and religion—a perspective which takes into account the fact that in all known cultures there has been an interaction of legal and religious values. In a sense everything *is* religion; and in a sense, everything *is* law—just as everything is time and everything is space. Man is everywhere and always confronting an unknown future, and for that he needs faith in a truth beyond himself, or else the community will decline, will decay, will fall backward.

Similarly, man is everywhere and always confronting social conflict, and for that he needs legal institutions, or else the community will dissolve, will break apart. These two dimensions of life are in tension—yet neither can be fulfilled without the other. Law without faith degenerates into legalism; this indeed is what is happening today in many parts of America and of the Western world. Faith without law, as I shall try to show in a subsequent chapter, degenerates into religiosity. We must begin with these basic cross-cultural truths if we are to succeed in understanding what history requires of us here and now.

II.

● The Influence of Christianity on the Development of Western Law

Thus far we have considered religion and law in their universal aspects. In all societies, even the most sophisticated, there are shared beliefs in transcendent values, shared commitments to an ultimate purpose, a shared sense of the holy; and in all societies, even the most rudimentary, there are structures and processes of social ordering, established methods of allocating rights and duties, a shared sense of the just. These two dimensions of social life are in tension: the prophetic and mystical sides of religion challenge, and are challenged by, the structural and rational sides of law. Yet each is also a dimension of the other. Every legal system shares with religion certain elements—ritual, tradition, authority, and universality—which are needed to symbolize and educate men's legal emotions. Otherwise law degenerates into legalism. Similarly, every religion has within it legal elements, without which it degenerates into private religiosity.

This, admittedly, is a very long-range view of our common humanity. When we look more closely, we see that mankind has many different religions and many different kinds of law, each religion bearing the stamp of a particular community of faith and each kind of law bearing the stamp of a particular social order. It is the religious and legal beliefs and practices of a particular society, and not some ideal religion and some ideal law, that give the members of that society their faith in the future, on the one hand, and their social cohesion, on the other. And the religious and legal beliefs and practices of a particular community are always intimately related to the unique experience of that community, its unique history.

And so when we turn from universal aspects of the interrelations of religion and law to the interrelations of particular religions and particular legal systems, we turn inevitably from the study of human nature to the study of history—that is, to the study of the realization of human nature in social experience. The philosopher asks timeless questions: What is religion? What is law? But these questions are unanswerable until we have made them timely and specific. Not "What is the nature of man?" but "What am I, my God? What is my nature?" asked St. Augustine.[1] Similarly, the social scientist must ask: Who are we? How have we come into being? What experiences have formed our character? In what direction are we heading? What alternatives confront us? For the "nature" of "man" in "society" is

only to be found in the living deposits of remembered social experience, such as religion and law, and these exist everywhere not in abstraction but in the history of the communities in which we live. It is in this sense that Ortega was right in saying that man has no nature, he has only a history.[2]

In the perspective of our own Western history, the religious dimensions of law appear first as a succession of challenges made by the Christian church in the various stages of its development—and increasingly, in the last two centuries, by secular religions derived from Christianity—to adapt legal institutions to human needs. The basic theme of the story is Jesus' ringing cry, "The sabbath was made for man, not man for the sabbath!" But the opposite theme cannot be suppressed: human needs become identified with the institutions of the religion itself, and the new legal institutions created to serve man acquire an authority independent of their purposes. And so the struggle must be repeated. Yet the memory of past victories gives a basis for hope that we may come closer to our goals; and behind the memory and the hope is a faith that the historical enterprise itself—including both religious history and legal history —is part of some great plan of salvation for man. This, in any event, is Christian historiography carried over from Judaism, and in recent centuries carried over to many of the secular religions that have come to dominate us, including both the religion of democracy and the religion of socialism.[3]

Historical Jurisprudence in a Christian Perspective

For Judaism, the center of gravity of human history is the history of the Jewish people and of the Judaic law that binds it to God and its members to each other; whereas for Christianity, the church from the time of St. Paul, though conceived to be a historical continuation of the Jewish people, was intended to embrace all other peoples as well, each with its own law. Therefore a new law was required within the church itself, as a religious community, to govern its relationships with God as well as the relationships of its members with each other; also new attitudes and policies were required with respect to the secular law by which individual Christians were governed in their nonreligious activities and by which the church as a whole was governed in its relationships with "the world."

In the first age of the church, the most striking fact about the secular law—the law of the Roman Empire—was that it altogether prohibited Christian worship. The church was illegal: to survive, it had to go underground —literally—into the catacombs. Thus the first principle of Christian jurisprudence, established by historical experience, was the principle of civil disobedience: laws that conflict with Christian faith are not binding in conscience. This had had its counterpart in Jewish history as well—for example, in the resistance to the worship of Baal, the story of Daniel's disobedience to King Darius, and refusals to place statues of the Roman emperors in the synagogues. There was, however, a dif-

ference: as Roman citizens, disobedient Christians were defying the laws of their own people. This fact had a considerable significance for the future, when the Christian church became part of the political establishment and individual Christians were confronted with unconscionable laws enacted by their own, not pagan but Christian, rulers—laws that were often imposed in the name of the church itself. People could not forget that the Christian era began with the assertion of a moral right—indeed, a duty—to violate a law that conflicts with God's will. This right and duty, reasserted in our own time by such men as Martin Luther King and the Berrigan brothers, is one of the foundations of our constitutional law of freedom of speech.[4]

With the conversion of the Roman emperors to Christianity in the fourth century, the church came to operate within the power structure. Now it faced a quite different aspect of the question of the relationship between law and religion—namely, whether the emperor's acceptance of the Christian faith had anything positive to contribute to his role as a legislator. The answer given by history was that the Christian emperors of Byzantium considered it their Christian responsibility to revise the laws, as they put it, "in the direction of greater humanity."[5] Under the influence of Christianity, the Roman law of the postclassical period reformed family law, giving the wife a position of greater equality before the law, requiring mutual consent of both spouses for the validity of a marriage, making divorce more difficult

(which at that time was a step toward women's liberation!), and abolishing the father's power of life or death over his children; reformed the law of slavery, giving a slave the right to appeal to a magistrate if his master abused his powers and even, in some cases, the right to freedom if the master exercised cruelty, multiplying modes of manumission of slaves, and permitting slaves to acquire rights by kinship with freemen; and introduced a concept of equity into legal rights and duties generally, thereby tempering the strictness of general prescriptions. Also the great collections of laws compiled by Justinian and his successors in the sixth, seventh, and eighth centuries were inspired in part by the belief that Christianity required that the law be systematized as a necessary step in its humanization. These various reforms were, of course, attributable not only to Christianity, but Christianity gave an important impetus to them as well as providing the main ideological justification. Like civil disobedience, law reform "in the direction of greater humanity" remains a basic principle of Christian jurisprudence derived from the early experience of the church.

In contrast to the Byzantine emperors, who inherited the great legal tradition of pagan Rome, the rulers of the Germanic, Slavic, and other peoples of Europe during roughly the same era (from the fifth to the tenth centuries) presided over a legal regime consisting chiefly of primitive tribal customs and rules of the blood feud. It is more than coincidence that the rulers of many of

the major tribal peoples, from Anglo-Saxon England to Kievan Russia, after their conversation to Christianity promulgated written collections of tribal laws and introduced various reforms, particularly in connection with family law, slavery, and protection of the poor and oppressed, as well as in connection with church property and the rights of clergy.[6] The Laws of Alfred (about A.D. 890) start with a recitation of the Ten Commandments and excerpts from the Mosaic law; and in restating and revising the native Anglo-Saxon laws Alfred includes such great principles as: "Doom [i.e., judge] very evenly; doom not one doom to the rich, another to the poor; nor doom one to your friend, another to your foe."

The church in those centuries, subordinate as it was to emperors, kings, and barons, sought to limit violence by establishing rules to control blood feuds; and in the tenth and eleventh centuries the great Abbey of Cluny, with its branches all over Europe, even had some success in establishing the so-called Peace of God, which exempted from warfare not only the clergy but also the peasantry, and the so-called Truce of God, which prohibited warfare on the weekends.[7] Here, too, are influences of religion on law that have bearing for our time.

Nevertheless, despite the reforms and innovations of Christian kings and emperors, the prevailing law of the West remained—prior to the twelfth century—the law of the blood feud, and of trial by battle, and by ordeals of fire and water, and by ritual oaths. There were no

professional judges, no professional lawyers, no law books, either royal or ecclesiastical. Custom reigned—tribal custom, local custom, feudal custom. In the households of kings and in the monasteries there was civilization to a degree; but without a system of law it was extremely difficult to transmit civilization from the centers to the localities. To take one example: the church preached that marriage is a sacrament which cannot be performed without the consent of the spouses, but there was no effective system of law by which the church could overcome the widespread practice of arranging marriages between infants. And not only were civilized values crushed by a hostile environment, but the church itself was under the domination of the same environment: lucrative and influential clerical offices were bought and sold by feudal lords, who appointed brothers and cousins to be bishops and priests.

In the latter part of the eleventh and first part of the twelfth century, there took place in the West a great revolution which resulted in the formation of a visible, corporate, hierarchical church, a legal entity independent of emperors, kings, and feudal lords, and subordinate to the absolute monarchical authority of the bishop of Rome. This was the Papal Revolution, of whose enormous significance medieval historians both inside and outside the Catholic Church are becoming increasingly aware.[8] It led to the creation of a new kind of law for the church as well as new kinds of law for the various secular kingdoms.

Previously the relationship between the spiritual and secular realms had been one of overlapping authorities, with emperors and kings (Charlemagne and William the Conqueror, for example) calling church councils and promulgating new theological doctrine and ecclesiastical law, and with popes, archbishops, bishops, and priests being invested in their offices by emperors, kings, and lords. In 1075, however, Pope Gregory VII proclaimed the complete political and legal independence of the church and at the same time proclaimed his own supreme political and legal authority over the entire clergy of Western Christendom.[9] It took forty-five years of warfare between the papal and the imperial parties—the Wars of Investiture—and in England it took the martyrdom of Thomas Becket before the papal claims were established (albeit with some substantial compromises).

The now visible, hierarchical, corporate Roman Catholic Church needed a systematic body of law, and in the twelfth and thirteenth centuries this was produced—first in a great treatise written about 1140 by the Italian monk Gratian and eighty years later, after a succession of jurist-popes had promulgated hundreds of new laws, by Pope Gregory IX in his Decretals of 1234. The Decretals remained the basic law of the Roman Church until 1917.

Of course there had been ecclesiastical canons long before Gratian, but they consisted of miscellaneous scattered decisions, decrees, teachings, etc., mostly of a theological nature, pronounced by various church coun-

cils and individual bishops, and occasionally gathered in chronologically arranged collections. There were also traditional procedures in ecclesiastical tribunals. However, there was no systematized body of ecclesiastical law, criminal law, family law, inheritance law, property law, or contract law, such as was created by the canonists of the twelfth and thirteenth centuries. The canon law of the later Middle Ages, which only today, eight centuries later, is being called into question by some leading Roman Catholics themselves,[10] was the first modern legal system of the West, and it prevailed in every country of Europe. The canon law governed virtually all aspects of the lives of the church's own army of priests and monks and also a great many aspects of the lives of the laity. The new hierarchy of church courts had exclusive jurisdiction over laymen in matters of family law, inheritance, and various types of spiritual crimes, and in addition it had concurrent jurisdiction with secular courts over contracts (whenever the parties made a "pledge of faith"), property (whenever ecclesiastical property was involved—and the church owned one-fourth to one-third of the land of Europe), and many other matters.

The canon law did not prevail alone, however. Alongside it there emerged various types of secular law, which just at this very time, in the twelfth and thirteenth centuries, began to be rationalized and systematized. In about 1100, the Roman law of Justinian, which had been virtually forgotten in the West for five centuries, was

rediscovered. This rediscovery played an important part in the development of the canon law, but it also was seized upon by secular rulers who resisted the new claims of the papacy. And so in emulation of the canon law, diverse bodies of secular law came to be created by emperors, kings, great feudal lords, and also eventually in the cities and boroughs that emerged in Europe in the twelfth and thirteenth centuries, as well as among merchants trading in the great international fairs. The success of the canon law stimulated secular authorities to create their own professional courts and a professional legal literature, to transform tribal, local, and feudal custom, and to create their own rival legal systems to govern feudal property relations, crimes of violence, mercantile transactions, and many other matters.

Thus it was the church that first taught Western man what a modern legal system is like. The church first taught that conflicting customs, statutes, cases, and doctrines may be reconciled by analysis and synthesis. This was the method of Abelard's famous *Sic et Non* (*Yes and No*), which lined up contradictory texts of Holy Scriptures—the method reflected in the title of Gratian's *Concordance of Discordant Canons*. By this method the church, in reviving the study of the obsolete Roman law, transformed it by transmuting its complex categories and classifications into abstract legal concepts. These techniques were derived from *the principle of reason* as understood by the theologians and philosophers of the twelfth century as well as by the lawyers.

The church also taught *the principle of conscience*—in the corporate sense of that term, not the modern individualist sense: that the law is to be found not only in scholastic reason but also in the heart of the lawgiver or judge. The principle of conscience in adjudication was first stated in an eleventh-century tract which declared that the judge must judge himself before he may judge the accused, that he must, in other words, identify himself with the accused, since thereby (it was said) he will know more about the crime than the criminal himself knows.[11] A new science of pleading and procedure was created in the church courts, and later in secular courts as well (for example, the English Chancery), "for informing the conscience of the judge." Procedural formalism was attacked. (In 1215 the Fourth Lateran Council effectively abolished trials by ordeal throughout Europe by forbidding clergy to participate in them.) The right to direct legal representation by professional lawyers and the procedure for interrogation by the judge according to carefully worked out rules were among the new institutions created to implement the principle of conscience. Conscience was associated with the idea of the equality of the law, since in conscience all litigants are equal; and from this came equity—the protection of the poor and helpless against the rich and powerful, the enforcement of relations of trust and confidence, and the granting of so-called personal remedies such as injunctions. Equity, as we noted earlier, had been part of the postclassical Roman law as well,

but it was now for the first time made systematic, and special procedures were devised for invoking and applying it.

And so the church sought both to legalize morality and to moralize legality; it took legal jurisdiction over sins, and it influenced the secular law to conform to moral principles. As in ancient Israel, the distinction between law and morality was minimized. On the one hand, standards of right and wrong were reinforced by legal procedures and legal sanctions; on the other hand, a divine righteousness was attributed to legal standards which they by no means always had. Universal celibacy of the priesthood, for example, was made a legal requirement in the eleventh century in order to insulate the clergy from clan and feudal politics, but it acquired an aura of sanctity that made it survive long after it had ceased to be necessary. The law of heresy is another example of the evil of confusing immorality with illegality. Excommunication for disobedience to ecclesiastical authority was a legal remedy which could deprive a person of his entire moral security.

There was, however, an important difference between medieval Christendom and ancient Israel in this regard: in medieval Christendom there was a conflict of jurisdictions between church and state, a coexistence and rivalry of diverse legal systems within each nation and a coexistence and rivalry of diverse nations within the church. The sanctity which a visible, hierarchical, corporate church could give to its law was challenged by the fact

61

that each person in Christendom lived not only under church law but also under several secular legal systems —royal law, feudal law, local law, merchant law, and others. Each of the secular legal systems also claimed sanctity; and that sanctity, too, was challenged—by the other secular legal systems as well as by ecclesiastical law. This pluralism of legal systems has remained a dominant feature of Western law, despite the inroads of nationalism and of positivism since the Protestant Reformation. In all countries of the West today, including the United States, every person lives under more than one legal system. We live not only under national law but also under international law; and we may invoke international legal custom as well as treaties and conventions and even declarations of the United Nations to challenge the acts of our national authorities. Also, we in America live under both state and federal law, and may run from one to the other for protection; we live under both statute law and constitutional law and may invoke concepts of "due process" and "equal protection" to oppose the will of the legislature; we live under both strict law and equity—under the rule and under the discretion to depart from the rule in exceptional cases. The coexistence of diverse legal systems within the same polity gives a legal foundation to the concept of the supremacy of law; political power is always subject to legal challenge, unless the ruler has seized control of *all* the available legal systems.

The medieval church also taught *the principle of the*

growth of the law—that legal doctrines and legal institutions are to be consciously based on past authority and yet are to be consciously adapted to the needs of the present and future. The canon lawyers worked out new rules and doctrines on the basis of Justinian, the Bible, the church fathers, Aristotle, Germanic customs; they revered the authoritative texts, but they glossed them and then glossed the glosses. The concept of organic growth helped to reconcile stability with flexibility. Just as the great Gothic cathedrals were built over centuries and had budgets projected for a thousand years, so the great law texts were constructed and reconstructed with eyes both to the past and to the future. And indeed they have survived: the reforms now taking place in the Roman Catholic Church are in part an effort to build once again on the legal foundations of the twelfth and thirteenth centuries. But more than that, the canon laws —of marriage, of inheritance, of torts, of crime, of contracts, of property, of equity, of procedure—have entered into the secular legal systems of the West, as has the principle of growth itself, with the result that there has in fact been created a common language of Western law, a Western legal tradition capable of organic development.

The Lutheran Reformation broke the medieval dualism of two kinds of official hierarchy, two kinds of official legal systems—that of the church and that of the secular authorities—by delegalizing the church. Where Lutheranism succeeded, the church came to be conceived

as invisible, apolitical, alegal; and the only sovereignty, the only law (in the political sense), was that of the secular kingdom or principality. It was just before this time, in fact, that Machiavelli invented the word "state" to apply to the purely secular political order. The Protestant reformers were in one sense Machiavellians in that they were skeptical of man's power to create a human law which would reflect eternal law, and they explicitly denied that it is the task of the church as such to develop human law. This Protestant skepticism made possible the emergence of a theory of law—legal positivism—which treats the law of the state as morally neutral, a means and not an end, a device for manifesting the policy of the sovereign and for securing obedience to it. But the secularization of law and the emergence of a positivist theory of law are only one side of the story of the contribution of the Protestant Reformation to the Western legal tradition. The other side is equally important: by freeing law from theological doctrine and from direct ecclesiastical influence, the Reformation enabled it to undergo a new and brilliant development. In the words of the great German jurist and historian Rudolf Sohm, "Luther's Reformation was a renewal not only of faith but also of the world: both the world of spiritual life and the world of law." [12]

The key to the renewal of law in the West from the sixteenth century on was the Protestant concept of the power of the individual, by God's grace, to change nature and to create new social relations through the

exercise of his will. The Protestant concept of the individual will became central to the development of the modern law of property and contract. Nature became property. Economic relations became contract. Conscience became will and intent. The last testament, which in the earlier Catholic tradition had been a means of saving souls by charitable gifts, became a means of controlling social and economic relations. By the naked expression of their will, their intent, testators could dispose of their property after death and entrepreneurs could arrange their business relations by contract. The property and contract rights so created were held to be sacred and inviolable, so long as they did not contravene conscience. Conscience gave them their sanctity. And so the secularization of the state, in the restricted sense of the removal of ecclesiastical controls from it, was accompanied by a spiritualization, and even a sanctification, of property and contract.

It is not true, therefore, that Protestantism placed no limits upon the political power of the absolute monarchs that ruled Europe in the sixteenth century. The development of positive law was conceived to rest ultimately upon the prince alone, but it was presupposed that in exercising his will he would respect the individual consciences of his subjects, and that meant respecting also their property and contract rights. This presupposition rested—precariously, to be sure—upon four centuries of history in which the church had succeeded in Christianizing law to a remarkable extent (given the level of

65

the cultural life of the Germanic peoples to begin with). Thus a Protestant positivism which separates law from morals, denies the lawmaking role of the church, and finds the ultimate sanction of law in political coercion nevertheless assumes the existence of a Christian conscience among the people and a state governed by Christian rulers.

We have spoken thus far of Protestantism primarily in its Lutheran form. A later form, Calvinism, has also had profound effects upon the development of Western law, and especially upon American law. The Puritans carried forward the Lutheran concept of the sanctity of the individual conscience and also, in law, the sanctity of the individual will as reflected in property and contract rights. But they added two new elements: first, a belief in the duty of Christians to reform the world—indeed, "reforming the world" was a specifically Puritan slogan;[13] and second, a belief in the local congregation, under its elected minister and elders, as the seat of truth—a "fellowship of active believers" higher than any political authority.[14] The active Puritan, bent on reforming the world, was ready to defy the highest powers of church and of state in asserting his faith, and he did so on grounds of individual conscience, also appealing to divine law, to the Mosaic law of the Old Testament, and to natural-law concepts embodied in the medieval legal tradition. As the early Christian martyrs founded the church by their disobedience to Roman law, so the seventeenth-century Puritans, includuding men like

Hampden, Lilburne, Udall, William Penn, and others, by their open disobedience to English law laid the foundations for the English and American law of civil rights and civil liberties as expressed in our respective Constitutions: freedom of speech and press, free exercise of religion, the privilege against self-incrimination, the independence of the jury from judicial dictation, the right not to be imprisoned without cause, and many other such rights and freedoms.[15] We also owe to Calvinist congregationalism the religious basis of our concepts of social contract and government by consent of the governed.[16]

The Jurisprudence of the Secular Religions

Puritanism in England and America, and Pietism, its counterpart on the European continent, were the last great movements within the institutional church to influence the development of Western law in any fundamental sense. In the eighteenth and nineteenth centuries both the Roman Catholic Church and the various Protestant denominations continued, of course, to exert pressures upon law in various directions. Undoubtedly, prophetic Christianity as such continued to play an extremely important part in effectuating law reform—for example in the abolition of slavery, in the protection of labor, and in the promotion of welfare legislation generally. And undoubtedly, on the other side, "organized religion" continued to support the status quo, whatever it happened to be. But the significant factor in this re-

67

gard—in the nineteenth century and even more so in the twentieth—has been the very gradual reduction of the traditional religions to the level of a personal, private matter, without public influence on legal development, while other belief systems—new secular religions ("ideologies," "isms")—have been raised to the level of passionate faiths for which people collectively are willing not only to die but also (which is harder) to live new lives.

It was the American and French Revolutions that set the stage for the new secular religions—that is, for pouring into secular political and social movements the religious psychology as well as many of the religious ideas that had previously been expressed in various forms of Catholicism and Protestantism. At first a kind of religious orthodoxy was preserved by means of a deistic philosophy —which, however, had little of that very psychology which is the heart of religious faith. What was religious, in fact, about the great revolutionary minds of the late eighteenth and nineteenth centuries—men like Rousseau or Jefferson—was not their belief in God but their belief in Man, individual Man, his Nature, his Reason, his Rights. The political and social philosophies that sprang from the Enlightenment were religions because they ascribed ultimate meaning and sanctity to the individual mind—and also, it must be added immediately, to the nation. The age of individualism and rationalism was also the age of nationalism: the individual was a citizen, and public opinion turned out to be not the opinion of man-

kind but the opinion of Frenchmen, the opinion of Germans, the opinion of Americans, and so forth.

Individualism, rationalism, nationalism—the Triune Deity of Democracy—found legal expression in the exaltation of the role of the legislature and the consequent reduction (except in the United States) of the law-creating role of the judiciary; in the freeing of individual actions from public controls, especially in the economic sphere; in the demand for codification of criminal and civil law; in the effort to make predictable the legal consequences of individual actions, again especially in the economic sphere. These "jural postulates" (as Roscoe Pound would have called them) [17] were considered to be not only useful but also just, and not only just but also part of the natural order of the universe. Life itself was thought to derive its meaning and purpose from these and related principles of legal rationality, whose sources in theological doctrines of natural law and of human reason are evident.

Liberal democracy was the first great secular religion in Western history—the first ideology which became divorced from traditional Christianity and at the same time took over from traditional Christianity both its sense of the sacred and some of its major values. But in becoming a secular religion, liberal democracy was very soon confronted with a rival: revolutionary socialism. And when, after a century of revolutionary activity throughout Europe, communism ultimately seized power in Russia in 1917, its doctrines had acquired the sanctity

69

of authoritative revelation and its leadership the charisma of high priests. Moreover, the Communist Party had the intimacy on the one hand, and the austerity on the other, of a monastic order. It is not accidental that during the purges after World War II loyal Communists in Europe used to say, "There is no salvation outside the Party."

The jural postulates of socialism, though they differ in many respects from those of liberal democracy, show a common ancestry in Christianity. The Soviet "Moral Code of the Builder of Communism," for example, which Soviet schoolchildren must learn by heart and which is taken as a basis for Soviet legal policy, contains such principles as: "conscientious labor for the good of society —he who does not work, neither shall he eat"; "concern on the part of everyone for the preservation and growth of public wealth"; "collectivism and comradely mutual assistance—one for all and all for one"; "honesty and truthfulness, moral purity, modesty, and unpretentiousness in social and personal life"; "an uncompromising attitude toward injustice, parasitism, dishonesty, careerism, and money-grubbing"; "an uncompromising attitude toward the enemies of communism"; "fraternal solidarity with the working people of all countries and with all people." [18] Soviet law is strkingly reminiscent of the Puritan code of the Massachusetts Bay Colony, the "Body of Liberties" of 1641, in its punishment of ideological deviation, idleness, and personal immorality.[19] In addition, the Soviet system places a very strong

emphasis on the educational role of law and on popular participation in legal proceedings and in law enforcement—through Comrades' Courts, People's Patrols, and placing persons in the care of the collective of the factory or the neighborhood. Moreover, this is done in the name of an eschatology which foresees the ultimate disappearance of coercion and of law itself as a communist society is created in which every person will treat every other—again, in the words of the Moral Code of the Builder of Communism—as "comrade, friend, and brother." It is by no means inconsistent with this utopian vision that strong measures of coercion and of formal law may be used to bring it about.

It is, of course, an exaggeration to compare the religious (or quasi-religious) character of political and social movements in the United States with that of communism in the Soviet Union. Yet in America and in all countries of the West the emotions that were once poured into traditional religions are now poured into secular movements: into party politics, welfare legislation, social reform, student revolt, the peace movement, women's liberation, ecology, and a host of others. Moreover, it is not only the emotional side of these movements that is of religious derivation; many of their ideas, as well, originated in Christianity and Judaism; and above all, their historical outlook is often similar—especially their faith in the future.

Meanwhile, Christianity itself is losing its public character, its political and legal dimension, and (in Jürgen

71

Moltmann's phrase) is becoming "privatized." [20] For the most part, people go to church as individuals, or as individual families, to gain spiritual nourishment to sustain them in activities and relationships that take place elsewhere.

We are thus confronted with a combination of a "religionless Christianity" [21] and what may be called a "Christianity-less religion." The question this raises for law is whether—and if so, how—such a combination can command sufficient authority to carry forward into a new age the great principles of Western jurisprudence established so painfully during the past two thousand years: the principle of civil disobedience, the principle of law reform in the direction of greater humanity, the principle of the coexistence of diverse legal systems, the principle of the conformity of law to a system of morals, the principle of the sanctity of property and contract rights based on intent, the principle of freedom of conscience, the principle of legal limitations on the power of rulers, the principle of the responsibility of the legislature to public opinion, the principle of predictability of the legal consequences of social and economic actions, as well as newer socialist principles of the priority of state interests and of public welfare. These principles may appear to some to be self-evident truths, and to others they may appear to be utilitarian policies, but for Western man as a whole they are, above all, historical achievements created mainly out of the experience of the Christian church in the various ages of its life: the underground

church of the first centuries, the theocratic state-church of Byzantium and of the early Middle Ages in the West, the independent transnational visible corporate church of the later Middle Ages, the invisible Lutheran church within the nation, the congregational church of Calvinism, and increasingly today the church of the private individual. These successive ages of the church have created the psychological basis, and many of the values, upon which the legal systems of democracy and socialism rest.

It is supposed by some—especially intellectuals—that fundamental legal principles, whether of democracy or of socialism, can survive without any religious or quasi-religious foundations on the basis of the proper political and economic controls and a philosophy of humanism. History, however, including current history, testifies otherwise: people will not give their allegiance to a political and economic system, and even less to a philosophy, unless it represents for them a higher, sacred truth. People will desert institutions that do not seem to them to correspond to some transcendent reality in which they believe—believe *in* with their whole beings, and not just believe *about*, with their minds. That is why countries of democracy and socialism that have abandoned traditional religions turn ultimately to religions of race, of country, or of class (or of all three). The intellectuals feel betrayed by this; they continually anticipate that people will develop a new style of consciousness, secular and rational like their own, but they do not realize that

their own belief in political and economic systems and in a humanist philosophy is equally transrational and equally self-interested—it is the religion of the intellectual.

I have attempted in these first two chapters to challenge the conventional view of law as something to be found primarily in lawbooks. Law is *not* primarily a collection of rules and of legal opinions applying rules to cases and of learned treatises and articles analyzing the ways in which rules are applied to cases. These are the residue of law in the minds of the experts, but its basic reality—in every society—consists in the drama of its continual enactment and reenactment; and that drama, with its ritual, its tradition, its authority, and its universality, manifests and effectuates not only legal principles and policies but also legal values, legal emotions. These, in turn, help to constitute the religious dimension of law, its sanctity.

These chapters are intended, secondly, to challenge the conventional view of law as the product solely of politics. Politics does, of course, give rise to legal rules and decisions; but unless people believe in the law, unless they attach a universal and ultimate meaning to it, unless they see it and judge it in terms of a transcendent truth, nothing will happen. The law will not work—it will be dead.

Thirdly, these chapters are meant to challenge the view that legal values are attributable primarily to man's rational faculties, his capacity to "figure out" sensible solu-

tions to his problems. Many of the basic principles of our law were, indeed, figured out and do, indeed, make sense—and we should be very glad of that; but they are real, and they command allegiance, also because they were fought for and won in the struggle of Western man to defend his faith and to adapt himself to new historical situations. If we lose our memory of the struggle which brought those principles into being, we shall not be able to properly evaluate them. We might disagree, for example, about the political wisdom of those of our contemporaries who practice civil disobedience and about the political wisdom of those who would have the government tolerate it; yet we should all agree that a court, in trying persons for violating laws which they sincerely believe to be unconscionable, ought to accept that belief as a mitigating rather than an aggravating circumstance —in deference to a heritage of more than two thousand years. Similarly, we might disagree about the wisdom of the legal principle that contracts should be kept—*pacta sunt servanda;* but we must recognize that to adopt a contrary principle, namely, that an agreement need not be kept if it proves disadvantageous to the weaker side, is to renounce more than four centuries of our religious and legal history. Here we may differ about the importance of that history—whether we should be bound by it in this particular matter—but we must recognize that the great passions which have created our heritage also create a presumption in favor of preserving it. The presumption of historical continuity is, to be sure, re-

buttable, but the burden of proof is on the proponents of change.

Finally, I have attempted to challenge the view that history is only a record of the past and not also a path to the future. Both Western law and Western religion treat history as a living tradition, a symbol of ongoingness. And both our legal and our religious traditions, by linking us with a past that antedates our political and economic ideology—antedates democracy as well as socialism—also link us with a future that transcends present ideological controversies. It is for this reason that the massive loss of confidence in law and in religion threatens our integrity as a people—threatens our whole past and therefore our whole future. One of the ways we must take to overcome that integrity crisis is to recover our sense of how, at various times in the history of Western man, the interaction of religion and law has made it possible to regenerate both.

III.

● Law as a Dimension of Religion

Our themes thus far have been, first, the dependence of law in all societies upon religious elements (ritual, tradition, authority, universality) to give it sanctity, and, second, the role of Christianity, and of secular religions derived from Christianity, in motivating and shaping the development of Western law. We have contended that the crisis of confidence in law which we are now experiencing in America and elsewhere can only be met and resolved if we recognize that law is not only a matter of social utility but also, and fundamentally, a part of the ultimate meaning and purpose of life, a matter involving man's whole being, including not only his reason and will but also his emotions and his faith.

But if it is true that we can only resolve the crisis of confidence in law by recourse to religion, what about the crisis of confidence in religion? To appeal to religion to rescue law in America today is like asking one drowning

man to save another. The question is, how can religion regain its own vitality?

Part of the answer, I believe, lies paradoxically in the recognition and restoration of its legal dimension. As law without religion loses its sanctity and its inspiration, so religion without law loses its social and historical character and becomes a purely personal mystique. Law (the process of resolving conflicts and creating channels of cooperation by allocation of rights and duties) and religion (a collective concern with and commitment to the ultimate meaning and purpose of life) are two different dimensions of human experience; but each is also a dimension of the other. They stand or fall together.

I do not speak of a union of law and religion, but of their dialectical interdependence. It is true that in some cultures, like those of ancient Israel and Islam, religion and law are identified with each other. A similar tendency may also be found in Hinduism and in many contemporary nonliterate cultures. The initial Buddhist revolt against Hinduism, like the initial Christian revolt against Judaism, was in part a revolt against the excessive sanctification of law and the excessive legalization of religion.

The revolt against legalism may go so far as to deny the religious value of any sort of law and to reject every legal element in religion. Buddhism in its purest form asks even the prince to give up his kingdom and to devote his life to seeking inner peace. Some Christian mystics espouse similar doctrines. Yet even in mysticism

a legal element is introduced once the mystics establish relations with each other and seek to hand on their beliefs and practices to the next generation. The Buddhist monk whose ultimate concern is his own achievement of Nirvana also considers it part of that same concern to maintain a school for training himself and others. American students and professors now involved in individual meditation, for example, have their Students' International Meditation Society, and their centers where they may consult about their practices, purchase their mantras, etc. Some fifteen hundred years ago St. Simeon Stylites sat on a high column for thirty years to express his rejection of the customs and laws of this world, but this was surely in itself a structuring of his religious values; moreover, he accepted the services of those who, with faith in his hermitic life, passed up food to him. And once mysticism moves from the hermitage to the monastery, it needs an even more elaborate law. It is no accident that the Western legal tradition founded by the canonists of the twelfth century had as one of its main sources of inspiration the penitential rules of monastic orders.

I would argue, then, that just as there is and must be in even the most legalistic religions a concern for man's inner spiritual life, so there is and must be in even the most mystical religions a concern for social order and social justice. In every religion there is and must be a legal element—indeed, two legal elements: one relating to the social processes of the community sharing the

79

particular religious faith, the other relating to the social processes of the larger community of which the religious community is a part.

The importance of this fact—that religion itself has legal dimensions—becomes apparent when we consider the strong antilegal tendencies of certain modern schools of religious thought. Indeed, it is said that in a large number of American seminaries today, both Protestant and Catholic, there is a deep-seated mistrust of any kind of law, a belief that structures and processes of social ordering are irrelevant and even alien to man's spiritual aspirations. A similar belief is surely widespread in our law schools, where law is viewed for the most part as a system of rules and techniques for resolving disputes and solving social problems but not as a response to man's ultimate concerns.

I should like to discuss three different doctrines that are offered by Christian theologians as justifications for the radical separation of religion and law—first, the doctrine that the only law which binds a Christian is the law of love ("love theology," as some have called it), leading to the belief that legal and ethical structures are always relative, always subordinate to the specific situation (so-called "situation ethics"); second, the doctrine that Christians should live by faith and not by law (I would call it "faith theology"), leading to the belief that the separate visible identity of the church should be dissolved and Christians should lose themselves in the "secular city" (so-called "religionless Chris-

tianity," which also takes the form of a Christian secularism); and third, antinomianism ("antilaw-ism" strictly so called—the doctrine that the resurrection of Christ introduced a new era of grace in which Christians, living at the end of time, are freed from all legal and moral bonds (I would call it a "hope theology")—a belief often associated with radical Protestantism but which today finds a new expression in the writings of some Roman Catholic theologians who are questioning from this position the justification for the church's system of canon law.

In addition, I shall discuss a fourth, nontheological doctrine, the antagonism to law on the part of what has been called the youth culture or counter culture of certain groups in America today, which preach and live a new secular apocalypticism based on a belief in the supremacy of spontaneity, enthusiasm, and love over all established procedures and structures for allocating rights and obligations.

Law and Love

Love theology proclaims that there is only one sacred commandment, to love God and man, and that true lovers in the Christian sense may disregard all other moral and legal rules. Love, it is said, is a free gift which cannot be made the subject of either moral or political law. Law, it is said, is abstract, objective, and impersonal, whereas love is concrete, subjective, and personal. Law generalizes, whereas love is concerned with the unique individual. Law is concerned with power,

with business, with secular affairs, whereas love is concerned with the Christian life. The true Christian, it is said, has no need of law; his rule is St. Augustine's: "Love, and do as you wish!" (*Dilige et quod vis fac.*) [1]

Such a contrast between love and law makes a caricature of both.

Surely no such contrast is made in either the Old or the New Testament. In the first place, the biblical commandments to "love God with all your heart, and all your soul, and all your strength" and to "love your neighbor as yourself" were not outside the Mosaic law but were integral parts of it, expressly stated in the Torah, and Jesus called them the summary, the very gist, of the Mosaic law. [2] This means that for both Judaism and Christianity love is conceived as the spirit of the law itself, and law—including its detailed rules of conduct as well as its broad principles of morality—is intended to be an incarnation of love. This is illustrated in the great passage in which Jesus, denouncing the lawyers and Pharisees, said, "Alas for you, lawyers and Pharisees, hypocrites! You pay tithes of mint and dill and cummin; but you have overlooked the weightier demands of the Law—justice, mercy, and good faith. It is these you should have practiced, without neglecting the others. Blind guides! You strain off a midge, yet gulp down a camel!" (Matt. 23:23.) In other words, Jesus did not divorce love from law, or law from justice and mercy, or the justice and mercy of law from its technical aspects —"mint and dill and cummin." Instead, he insisted on

82

interpreting *all* law in the light of its spirit and purpose —in the light of love—rather than literally and mechanically. Thus he healed on the sabbath, he ate with the Gentiles, and most important of all, he defied the Sanhedrin. But he did not concede that in doing these things he violated the Judaic law; on the contrary, he did them in the name of the law itself, of what the law was all about. "I have come," he said, "to fulfill the law."

The divorce of law from love rests on the misconception that the essence of law consists in its rules and that law may be defined, essentially, as a body of rules. This neglects the active, living qualities of law as a process of social ordering. Law as a living social institution, law in action, is as concrete, subjective, and personal as any other aspect of social life. A trial in court surely is no more abstract than a church service. There is nothing impersonal about putting a man in jail because he committed a burglary, or enjoining a school board from excluding black children from a high school, or awarding a man who has been run down by an automobile money damages to pay his hospital bills. Law is not only rules and concepts; law is also, and primarily, a set of relationships among people. Love of God and of neighbor, including the sacrificial love which Jesus preached and lived, is no more excluded from legal relationships than from any other type of human relationship. The contrast between law and love exaggerates the role of rules in

law and underestimates the role of decision and óf relationship.

It also misconceives the function of legal rules. Rules
are not a denial of our unique, individual personalities.
On the contrary, they are necessary to protect our unique,
individual personalities from capricious, arbitrary, and
oppressive action. It is true, of course, that they are
cast in terms of similarities among people; they treat
people as members of classes or categories. They must
do so in order to preserve the basic principle of law,
that like cases should be decided alike. But this is not
only a principle of justice; it is also a principle of love.
For it is not love to treat a person unequally with others
in a situation in which he ought to be treated equally.
It would not be love for a legislature or court or administrative body to require some persons to pay higher
taxes, for example, than others living in exactly the
same circumstances. It may well be love for a person
to give his property to another person who has a greater
need of it, but it would not be love for society to permit
that other person to take the property without permission.
Living, as we do, a common life of interaction with each
other, our personalities require—for love's sake—the protection of general principles impartially administered.

Moreover, equal treatment and the principles of the
generality and impartiality of law are not to be understood as a Procrustean bed to which everyone must be
fitted regardless of his actual size. This is the great fallacy
about the law which so many nonlawyers—and indeed,

some lawyers—share: that it is a mechanical system of fitting fact situations to rules. Of course, it may—and often does—degenerate into that; but it is not inherently that. Rules of law, like all linguistic utterances, derive their meaning from the context in which they are spoken or written. In court proceedings, for example, the parties appear; they and others testify; the personal qualities of all the participants in the proceeding are visible to each other; the evidence is weighed; judgments are formed as to how individual persons should be dealt with in the light of general policies. At every stage there is a balancing of rule and discretion. The danger in most cases actually lies more in subjectivity than in objectivity. Once again, it is a matter not only of justice but also of love that society does not permit the "concrete, subjective, and personal" factors to remain uncontrolled.

More, of course, is involved than court procedures, or even all legal procedures, including those of legislation and administration. What is involved is the nature of our membership in larger communities. The radical separation of church and state in the West has led ultimately to the Calvinist teaching that "every duty is owed to the state except love." Of course it is idolatrous to love an abstract political structure. But to put the family, the congregation, the neighborhood, the school, and other face-to-face groups on one side of the moral ledger, to be loved, and the larger communities to which we belong—city, region, race, nation, mankind—on the other side, to be served without love, by a mechanical,

bureaucratic structure of law, not only sterilizes law but also romanticizes love. Love may indeed express itself in uncontrolled outbursts of joyous feelings; but as soon as love extends beyond the intimate relations of a few people, it demands procedures and rules to do its work.

But law is not excluded from intimate personal relationships either. Even within the family, the loving way to regulate many matters is by law—by assignment of tasks among the members, fair hearing of disputes, consistency in giving rewards and punishments, insistence on keeping agreements, respect for each other's belongings, and other manifestations of the principles of equality, generality, impartiality, reciprocity. The social order maintained within the family differs from the social order maintained within the state in the extent to which it can dispense with formality. Its law is for the most part informal law, customary law, whereas the law of the modern state is for the most part formal law, enacted law. In both small and large communities, however, relationships of mutual interdependence and mutual support are regulated, in part, by processes for allocating rights and duties and thereby resolving conflicts and creating channels of cooperation.

Both law and love suffer from overdrawn distinctions between rule and application of rule, between act and person, between large social aggregations and face-to-face groups—distinctions which have great utility when understood to be relative but which are very dangerous when made absolute. The distinction is absolutized when

law is treated as a purely technical or mechanical system independent of its underlying purposes; the distinction is also absolutized when love is treated as a purely personal or *ad hoc* feeling independent of its social forms of expression.

The fallacy on both sides is apparent in current theories of "situation ethics," which would derive the solution to ethical questions from the particular situations in which the questions arise, situations to be approached with Christian love but otherwise subject to no moral rules.[3] "Love, and do as you wish." This is, of course, an understandable reaction against ethical systems that deduce detailed rules of conduct from religious doctrines and apply the rules according to rigid categories. In fighting against such "insidious legalism," contemporary theologians are surely justified in emphasizing that rules should not be made objects of idolatry but rather should be adapted to human and social needs. The reaction goes too far, however, when situations are treated as though they were subject to no rules whatever. It is interesting that the rule skepticism of contemporary theology has its almost exact counterpart in certain modern schools of jurisprudence, especially in so-called "legal realism," which doubts the validity of all legal rules and seeks to reach solutions on the basis of beneficial consequences in the particular case or, more profoundly, on the basis of the judge's sense of the character of the situation and of the rules immanent in it.

The chief fallacy in situation ethics or situation law

is the presupposition that the situation defines itself—
that it presents itself ready-made as a situation—whereas
in fact it is defined in part by the very rules that the
situation ethicist or the legal realist would prefer to
dispense with. The rules are an integral part of the
situation, as are the persons who are supposed to resolve
it—the judges or legislators or administrators or others.
It may be possible as a purely academic classroom exercise
to consider, quite independently of any rules and quite
independently of who the discussants happen to be,
whether, for example, in a particular concrete situation
a doctor should be permitted to take the life of a patient;
but if the question is presented in real life, in a hospital
or a courtroom or a legislature, one cannot possibly exclude the rules without also excluding the hospital administration or the judge or the legislators since they
derive their rights and duties in the matter from those
very rules. Indeed, one would have to exclude the case
itself, since it is only a case insofar as there are some
rules making it a case. And basically the same is true of
the situation as presented in the classroom as well: an
essential part of what makes it a situation is the rule that
homicide is unjustified under certain circumstances and
justified under others.

In short, to rule law out of social relations, whether in
society as a whole or in small groups, is to leave caprice,
arbitrariness, and oppression—not love. Love needs law.
Indeed, from both a Judaic and a Christian standpoint,
and from a humanist standpoint as well, this is law's

chief justification and also its chief purpose, namely, to help create conditions in which love may flourish.

This may be illustrated by some very elementary examples. The United States Constitution provides for freedom of speech as well as freedom of religious worship and religious teaching; this gives those who believe in love a fighting chance to circulate their message. The tax laws permit charitable deductions from income and thus encourage financial contributions to those who are in need. School laws make education compulsory and thus promote literacy, which in turn makes possible the reading of the Scriptures. The law which makes bigamy a punishable offense helps preserve women from certain forms of oppression and strengthens the family. The law of property and of credit transactions—the law of zoning and of urban renewal and the law of mortgages, for example—help (as in the case of Federal Housing Authority mortgages) to overcome wretched overcrowding in the cities. The law of contracts helps to create conditions of confidence in business dealings. There are many things wrong with these and other branches of law, but if they were taken away, love would be forced to operate in a social chaos. That law alone cannot create love is obviously true; that the operation of love in society demands law both as a preparation for love and as a vehicle for love is less obvious but equally true.

It will be asked: Is it really love that law thus helps to foster, or is it not just goodwill, decency? Is it the kind of sacrificial spirit that we associate with such words

as *caritas, agape,* or is it not just the maintenance of minimum standards of good behavior so as to serve our mutual self-interest? The question suggests—what is quite true—that law does not generally require sacrificial or heroic acts, and that even if it were to require such acts it could not compel people to have the sacrificial or heroic feelings that are supposed to accompany them. But this could be put another way: love does not ask law to require such acts or feelings—love would not be served by such legal requirements. Law serves love not by seeking to replace it but by creating a soil in which it may grow. The fact, for example, that the judge is impartial, that he listens to both sides of a case, that he opens his mind and heart to both plaintiff and defendant, is designed to exclude prejudice or hatred as a factor in deciding. This is what love demands. The judge must put himself in the position of the parties. Likewise, the recognition of the binding force of promises in contract law, the punishment of crime, the enforcement of obligations of trust and confidence, the compensation for harm caused by negligence—are the kinds of things love asks from law, in order to help eliminate mistrust, wrongdoing, fraud, insecurity, and the like. Law is not supposed to be love; but it is supposed to be love's reliable servant. This is far different from saying that love and law are opposed to each other in some ultimate sense.

Moreover, to say that the law does not require sacrificial love is not to say that such love is not often

90

required of the lawyer or judge or legislator or executive officer who is involved in the enterprise of making or enforcing the law—or of the citizen who observes it. The conscientious lawyer who is torn between his duty to his client and his duty to the court—for he is both the representative of the one and an officer of the other —has need of great integrity of mind and heart. We should recognize the devotion of sensitive lawyers who wrestle with intolerable spiritual dilemmas not of their own making. Similarly we should sing the heroism of those judges who risk the opprobrium and scorn of their communities by their adherence to law; one thinks especially of many judges in the Deep South who in the 1950s and 1960s conscientiously applied high-level principles concerning racial equality which their local communities rejected. Here, too, though in a different sense, law was the servant of love.[4]

Law and Faith

Like the contrast between law and love, the contrast between law and faith also underestimates the social dimension—and hence the legal dimension—of religion. However, "faith theology," unlike "love theology," is not so much concerned with how society as a whole should be structured (or not structured) or with how a person should relate to his neighbor as with how the religious community should be structured (or not structured) and how a person should relate to God.

Here we are taken back to Luther's doctrine of justi-

fication by faith and to his attack upon the canon law. The prince, Luther said, should rule by law since he serves and protects others, but the individual Christian "is a person to himself; he believes for himself and for no one else."[5] A Christian is therefore "justified," or made holy, by faith alone, although of course he ought also, as a secondary matter, to obey the "outward ordinances of God" (as well as those of the prince). Luther would have had little sympathy with modern love theology or with situation ethics; he categorically denied that the doctrine of justification by faith releases a man from the obligation to observe the Ten Commandments and all their ramifications in the moral law. Indeed, once faith makes a man a believer, Luther said, then "the works begin."[6] But it is faith that requires good works, not any ecclesiastical hierarchy. As a Christian is "a person to himself," so the church is an invisible community of Christians within the territory of the prince. The church cannot organize itself into an independent legal entity without offending God.

Thus if Luther were alive today, he might well have some sympathy for the faith theology of those who now attack the external forms of religion, the churches as separate entities, the self-identification of Christians in cults and in organizations. Dietrich Bonhoeffer, in particular, seems to carry forward the spirit of Luther when he pleads that Christianity should give up its institutional identity and its pietism and should "lose its life . . . in its service to and through the world."[7] Bonhoeffer's

"religionless Christianity" fully commits the individual Christian to the world in which he lives. He must lose himself in the interests and problems of his time. Man has "come of age" and should not cling to religion for support. This has led to the view that Christians should give up their churches and become part of "the secular city." [8]

Yet those who in the name of faith now call for a dissolution of ecclesiastical structures do not tell us how, without them, faith is to be kept alive within the religious community and transmitted to future generations. Moreover, they do not demonstrate—although they assume—that the law of religious communities, their processes of self-regulation, cannot effectively symbolize Christian faith. They disparage as being of only secondary ("penultimate") importance, or possibly less, the standards and procedures and ceremonies whereby members of churches are brought together for worship, for religious education, for mutual encouragement, and for social action—failing to recognize that these standards and procedures and ceremonies are potentially sacramental in quality. Shall the churches give up all laws and customs concerning baptism, confirmation, marriage, and burial? Shall they give up self-government by deacons, or vestry, or committees, or whatever other forms may be used in various denominations? Shall they give up the worship service? Shall they give up donations to those in need of them? Shall they give up

social action? Or should they not, on the contrary, try to restore the sacred quality of these things?

We do not need to resolve the intricacies of various theological doctrines of justification in order to know that faith requires not only individual works but also collective works, and that collective works embodied in law may have as much ultimate (and not merely penultimate) value as anything else a man may do. Even Luther, we should recall, taught that law has not only the negative value of calling men to repentance and deterring them by penalties but also the positive value of giving guidance to those who seek to serve God.[9] Nor is it contrary to Lutheranism (or to any other major interpretation of Christianity) to say, with Calvin, that the faithful man delights in the law, through which he not only gains wisdom but is also "excited to obedience."[10]

One may ask, quite properly, what law is being talked about here—the moral law of the Ten Commandments? The law of reason and of human nature written in the hearts of men? The law of the church? The various branches of secular law—contracts, torts, property, criminal law, corporation law, administrative law, constitutional law, and the rest? Does the faithful man delight in all of these? Yes, indeed—insofar as they teach wisdom and virtue. But here we should be quite specific. Faithful men should delight not only in broad moral principles such as those reflected in the Ten Commandments but also in such matters of secular law as impartial

adjudication of disputes, judicial review of the constitutionality of governmental acts, the rule that a person who negligently injures another should compensate for the harm he has caused, the presumption of innocence, the right of a man arrested by the police to have a judicial determination of the lawfulness of his detention, the interpretation of contracts according to the intent of the parties, the principle of equal protection regardless of race or creed, the concept of good faith—and a host of other legal institutions, practices, rights, rules, concepts, and values. These are not only matters of policy and utility; every one of them has its source in the moral order of the universe as that moral order has been culturally and historically experienced. At least so far as the American legal tradition is concerned, every one of these principles is biblical in justification if not in origin. For us as a historical people, they manifest God's purpose.

The crisis of religion in America today does not arise —as it did in Luther's time—from its excessive legalization; on the contrary, it is the decline in the institutional self-identification of religion and in its social forms of expression—it is the weakness of the churches as formal communities—that is a principal symptom if not a principal cause of the impotence of Christianity today. Religion in America is becoming the private affair of individuals seeking to be unburdened of their loneliness, a cult of personal peace of mind. As the German theologian Jürgen Moltmann put it after spending some time

in this country, Christianity seems to be nurturing a privatized personal existence, and in so doing it becomes assimilated into society and is left with little to say other than what the world wants to hear.[11] In fact many of our religious structures are collapsing—although religious sentiments are spreading. In these circumstances religionless Christianity only contributes to the danger of new Christianity-less religions—political and social faiths —which (in the prophetic words of William Butler Yeats) lack all conviction or, even worse, are only full of passionate intensity.

Law and Grace

The third contrast—the contrast of law with grace— builds on the contrast of law with love and the contrast of law with faith, but goes beyond them. In the words of St. John's Gospel, "For while the Law was given through Moses, grace and truth came through Jesus Christ" (John 1:17). This presupposes a faith in Jesus Christ as the supreme revelation of God and a total surrender to him beyond the requirements of the moral law, as well as a love which freely and without compulsion of the moral law does those acts which God desires. Jesus taught that such faith and such love are the keys to the kingdom of God. Even this, however, is not yet grace. Grace, according to the Christian teaching, is a gift of God to the community of the followers of the risen Christ who, living the Christian life of faith and love, have entered

96

into God's kingdom. The church is the communion of saints living the Christian life and eagerly waiting for the imminent return of Christ at the end of the world. This was the message especially of St. Paul, who taught that the church lives at the end of time in the era of grace. To some modern theologians, this means that it should live without law.

We may call this a "hope theology," since it rests on expectation of the impending manifestation of God's presence, which, it is said, frees the church from all profane purposes, all power, all compulsion, all secular activities, all business, and therefore all law. Living in anticipation of the imminent return of the Messiah, the church (it is thought by some) should live spontaneously and freely, without structures of authority, without enforceable rules of conduct, without a legal process.

The spiritual power of such a thoroughgoing antinomianism cannot be denied. It proclaims a self-conscious, identified Christian community that does not say what the world wants to hear, but fights the world with specifically Christian weapons—not only with faith and love but with an apocalyptic vision of the church living a Christian life in the end of time. Nevertheless, this theology rests on two basic errors. The first is the belief that the church can preserve its faith and love, and its Christian life, without its own structures of authority and its own procedures and norms for resolving conflicts and channeling cooperation—in a world, moreover, that in-

97

creasingly exerts pressure to absorb the church into secular structures, procedures, and norms. The second, even more fundamental error is the belief that grace excludes law. St. Paul is misquoted in this regard: he did not oppose grace to law but only to the *compulsion* of law, its sanctions. According to Paul, what the Mosaic law requires, the Christian will do freely—living, as he does, in grace in the last days before the return of the Messiah. If he does not do it, he must seek forgiveness, and it will be granted to him. In other words, for St. Paul grace involved not a rejection of the values of the Mosaic law but, on the contrary, an internalization of those values. "The [Mosaic] law is in itself holy," he stated, "and the commandment is holy, just, and good" (Rom. 7:12). Although Paul recognized another, still higher realm of faith and of grace, nevertheless the law remained for him an essential part of God's plan of salvation.

Similarly in the Fourth Gospel, the contrast drawn between the law given by Moses and the grace and truth that came with Jesus Christ must be understood (as C. H. Dodd has shown) in the light of Rabbinic Judaism, which taught that grace and truth (*chesed v-emes*) are the very essence of the law. What St. John is saying is that Moses proclaimed the law but Jesus embodies its very essence—"in him the spirit of it is made flesh." [12]

The concept that grace excludes law no more withstands analysis than does the concept that law is dis-

solved in love or made irrelevant by faith. All three concepts err in underestimating the God-givenness of such basic legal values as equality of treatment, impartial adjudication, reciprocity of obligations, social responsibility, and many others—values which Jesus summed up in the words justice, mercy, good faith. Without them, love and faith and hope are deprived of their social context; they are up in the air.

We do not overlook the tensions between law on the one hand and love, faith, and grace on the other. Love or faith may require a person to violate the law; grace operates outside the legal order and may intervene in a way that can be justified by no legal process. Law is deliberate; it takes time, whereas love, faith, and grace may be spontaneous and immediate. Religion is concerned with a man's whole being in a way that law is not. Yet a man's whole being includes his life as a member of the communities in which he lives. To be sure, one cannot simply transpose religious counsels of personal perfection into social and political life: this is the fallacy of many who in the 1920s and 1930s preached the "social gospel." Yet the neo-orthodox reaction of the 1930s and 1940s was often guilty of the opposite fallacy; for society, although it cannot operate on the basis of personal morality, is nevertheless not amoral, but rather operates on the basis of social morality. What we have argued here is that personal morality needs social morality —including legal morality—if it is to be effective in society.

Law and the Youth Culture

There is a striking parallel to antinomianism—antagonism to law—in the so-called youth culture of America today. Partly within traditional Christianity, but largely outside it, a new "consciousness" is proclaimed—a faith —which replaces law with love and maintains the apocalyptic hope that thereby a revolution will take place in the life-style not only of individuals, but of the nations of the world.[13] New forms of dress, new rituals of dance, of music, and of drugs, a new literature, and many other new symbols have been adopted by hundreds of thousands—perhaps millions—of American youth in order to make visible the new creed. Under attack are the traditional middle-class values of American society: in Charles Reich's words, "power, success, status, acceptance, popularity, achievements, rewards, excellence, and the rational, competent mind." These values are seen as empty, joyless, and fundamentally destructive. They are the values of legalism. Those who adhere to them, says Professor Reich (himself a teacher of property law), "want nothing to do with dread, awe, wonder, mystery, accidents, failure, helplessness, magic"—the experience of which is necessary if the "self" is not to be alienated and impoverished.[14]

One may wholeheartedly support the affirmation of spontaneity, joy, beauty, self-discovery, togetherness, love, and yet question how it is to be realized—and not only realized in a practical sense, but manifested, incarnated, made real in a spiritual sense—without structures or

100

processes, without norms, without a rational and just social order at least among those who embrace the revolutionary credo. Indeed, the hundreds of communes that have sprung up, where the new consciousness is being lived out most dramatically, have foundered again and again for lack of a sense of law. They find that faith, love, and hope will not raise crops and milk cows or, indeed, maintain peace in the commune unless they find expression in rules and procedures for the division of work, for family responsibility, for the sharing of property, for education of the members, and the like. And so the middle-class values and the "rational, competent mind" return—hopefully, however, not as ends in themselves but as servants of justice and of love and hopefully in forms expressive of the highest aims of the community. For the mistake is to suppose that law is external to man, that it is not part of his whole being, that it is extraneous to love, to faith, to grace; this is what leads to legalism on the one hand and religiosity, or sentimentality, on the other.

The youth culture, like the New Left, the peace movement, women's liberation, and other similar contemporary social movements, and indeed like democracy, socialism, and all the great ideologies and "isms" of the West, is derived ultimately from Christianity and cannot survive if it rejects the basic implications of Christianity, one of which is the affirmation of law as a dimension of the universe and as a dimension of man's spiritual life.[15] The same is true, of course, of the churches themselves:

they will not survive if they do not find institutional structures and processes that effectively communicate Christian values. This is not just a question of a new liturgy; it is a question of forms of congregational living, processes of self-regulation as a community, rights and duties of members interacting with each other to achieve common purposes. Moreover, the community cannot ignore the law of the whole society of which it is a part: it must concern itself with housing law, welfare law, family law, drug control, criminal law, the courts, and many other separate aspects of the secular law, attempting to make use of the law in fulfilling its own mission and working for law reform as part of that mission.

That law is a dimension of love and faith, and a dimension of grace itself, is a basic, if neglected, concept of both Judaism and Christianity, both of which proclaim that God is himself a lawgiver and judge and, moreover, that his laws and judgments are a wonderful thing, a thing of grandeur and joy, a blessing for mankind. This is expressed throughout both the Old Testament and the New. So the psalmist sings, in words that are still repeated today in every single denomination of both the Jewish and the Christian faiths:

> Let the rivers clap their hands,
>   let the hills sing aloud together
> before the Lord; for he comes
>   to judge the earth.
> He will judge the world with righteousness
>   and the peoples with justice. (Ps. 98:8-9)

Throughout the psalms, God's righteousness and justice are equated with his steadfast love. According to Isaiah, his judgment is "to pursue justice and champion the oppressed," to relieve the fatherless, to plead for the widow (Isaiah 1:17). And he commands his people also to judge righteously. We read in Deuteronomy: "You are to hear the cases that arise among your kinsmen and judge fairly between man and man whether fellow-countryman or resident alien. You must be impartial and listen to high and low alike: have no fear of man, for judgment belongs to God" (Deut. 1:16-17). The prophets take up this theme. When God judges it is not for death but for life.[16] And their messianic vision, like that of the psalmist, is that God will send a King who "shall rule wisely, maintaining law and justice in the land" (Jer. 23:5). For Jeremiah, God's judgment, his law, means the regeneration of the whole society.[17] And for Micah, as for Isaiah, in the last days, when "out of Jerusalem comes the word of the Lord; he will be judge among many peoples . . . and they shall beat their swords into mattocks" (Micah 4:3).

There is, of course, another side to God's judgments: they requite wickedness with suffering. Sins must be punished. Yet this is to be viewed as inevitable rather than as desirable—a necessary means of stamping out evil. "The law must keep its promises."[18] Strangely enough, it is the New Testament, not the Old, that introduces the concept of eternal hellfire.

In the New Testament it is Christ to whom God's

authority to execute judgment has been given. Now that the end is at hand, the followers of Christ should refrain from acts of retribution or condemnation. "Pass no judgment, and you will not be judged" (Matt. 7:1). "Why do you pass judgment on your brother? . . . why do you hold your brother in contempt? we shall all stand before God's tribunal" (Rom. 14:10). At the same time, as we have seen, Jesus placed a very high value on justice between man and man, on good faith, on obedience, on social responsibility, on "always treat[ing] others as you would like them to treat you" (Matt. 7:12). And St. Paul said not only that the Mosaic law is sacred but that obedience to all just laws is required by conscience and that the state itself is "God's agent working for your good" (Rom. 13:4).

One may ask what these hymns of praise to law have to do with the laws of the Commonwealth of Massachusetts or the provisions of the United States Code or with the mass of rules and concepts taught in our law schools under the headings of torts, contracts, property, corporations, taxation, antitrust law, and the like; or with the trial of the Chicago Seven, or sending a man to prison for five years for smoking marijuana, or for violating the Selective Service Act; or with laws discriminating against the poor, or against racial minorities, or against women. Does Christianity teach that all this law is sacred, that it is part of God's plan of salvation for man, that it incarnates religious values? Of course, similar questions may be asked about faith, hope, and love as they exist

actually in the lives of men with thousands of different sets of values and ways of life—unjust and just, cruel and kind, superstitious and rational. Is the man fulfilling the gospel who, with love in his heart for all mankind and faith in God, orders the bombing of civilians in Vietnam or in Dresden? It is easy enough to say, Obviously not! Neither is the man who demagogically votes for appropriations for the poor in order to advance his own selfish interests. Clearly, morality requires that we do the right thing for the right reason—not the wrong thing for the right reason or the right thing for the wrong reason.

But such counsels of perfection will not answer the questions we are asking: first, how human justice—which is generally tainted with injustice—can be opened to the inspiration of values held to be sacred; and second, how human faith, hope, and love—which are generally tainted with disillusionment, despair, and apathy—can be made manifest in social institutions which, in St. Paul's phrase, are there to serve God for our benefit.

The first of these questions was the theme of chapters one and two; the second has been the theme of this chapter—namely, that contemporary religious thought must incorporate the dimension of law into its concept of the sacred, and contemporary religious experience must be incarnated in legal structures and processes, both within religious communities and in the larger society of which they are a part, if the vitality of religion is to be restored in America and in the world.

105

IV.

⬤ Beyond Law, Beyond Religion

In Dostoevsky's famous legend of the Grand Inquisitor, Jesus Christ returns to sixteenth century Spain and is recognized by the Grand Inquisitor, who tells him that he should not have refused the Devil's offer of economic, political, and ideological power. "In place of the rigid ancient law," the Grand Inquisitor says to Jesus, "[Thou hast said that] man must hereafter with free heart decide for himself what is good and what is evil, having only Thy image before him as his guide." But man cannot exist without bread, without rulers, and without miracle and mystery and authority; so the Church, he says, for the sake of man, has "corrected Thy work." Christ says nothing.

This story is usually misunderstood—perhaps because it is taken out of its context—as representing Dostoevsky's own conception of Christ and the betrayal of him by organized religion. But one must recall that Dostoevsky puts this "poem in prose" in the mouth of Ivan Karamazov, the rationalist, the Westernizer, who tells it

to his brother Alyosha to explain why he, Ivan, cannot accept a world in which innocent people suffer and why he has decided to give God back his "entrance ticket" to life. Alyosha, who in the novel stands for Russian mysticism and compassion, rejects the legend. "That's absurd!" he says. "That's not the idea of [freedom] in the Orthodox Church. . . . That's Rome, and not even the whole of Rome, it's false—those are the worst of the Catholics, the Inquisitors, the Jesuits." Alyosha refuses to accept Ivan's theory of an irreducible antithesis between spiritual freedom and sacrificial love, on the one hand, and the economic, political, and ideological needs of man, on the other. He refuses to believe that Christ stands for a truth that is beyond man's capacity to serve or to blame God for injustice and suffering.

Nevertheless, Alyosha offers no philosophical alternative to Ivan's dilemma. Instead, Dostoevsky starts a new chapter, entitled "The Russian Monk," in which a manuscript written by Alyosha tells the story of his mentor, Father Zossima, who as a young man turned from a frivolous and wicked life to one of brotherhood, service, and prayer. The answer to Ivan is the real life of a saintly monk. But apparently Dostoevsky himself was not wholly satisfied with this solution. Alyosha's manuscript about Father Zossima is incomplete. Alyosha himself plans to leave Father Zossima and "go out into the world." Indeed, Dostoevsky made several unsuccessful attempts to write a sequel to *The Brothers Karamazov* which would tell the story of Alyosha "out in the world." [1]

Dostoevsky rejected the Western concept of the dualism of religion and law; instead he called for the spiritualization of law or, as he put it, "the transformation of the State into the Church," [2] that is, the conversion of economic, political, and social institutions into a universal community characterized by spiritual freedom and sacrificial love. In this he saw beyond the era of Western rationalism to a time when men would not be willing to accept the antithesis of the spiritual versus the secular, of faith and love versus science and politics, of religion (or as it is now often called, ideology) versus legal processes of social ordering. That time came for Russia a generation after Dostoevsky's vision, in 1917, though in a way wholly the opposite of that which Dostoevsky had hoped for. And in a still different way it is coming today for America. The separation of church and state in the sense in which that phrase is understood in American constitutional law is, indeed, becoming more and more absolute, but this only means that the state itself is becoming more and more sanctified by the secular religon of the American Way of Life.[3]

The era of the dualism of spiritual and secular authorities is the era that began nine hundred years ago in Europe when new sophisticated legal systems were constructed out of the revival of Roman law, when new sophisticated theological systems were constructed out of the revival of Greek philosophy, and when the modern Roman Catholic Church was constructed as a visible, corporate hierarchical entity independent of all secular

109

authorities; the era that was renewed four hundred fifty years later by the Protestant Reformation and the accompanying rise of the European system of secular states; the era that was thereafter transformed successively by the English Revolution of the seventeenth century, the American and French Revolutions of the late eighteenth century, and the Russian Revolution of November, 1917. Since the Reformation, each of the great European revolutions—and for these purposes one must place Russia among the European nations—was fought in part to transfer some of the legal and ideological authority of the church to the state and to create new divisions between religion and law.

It is precisely this era that after nine centuries reached its denouement in the two world wars and the world revolution of the twentieth century. These catastrophic events of our time expose the insolvency of the nine-hundred-year-old tradition of the radical separation of religion and law—its apparent incapacity to prevent either the decay of our social, economic, and political life within the nation-state, on the one hand, or, on the other, the breakdown of international relations and the threatened self-destruction of mankind by war.

The Age of Synthesis

What is coming to an end is not only a particular political and ecclesiastical tradition, a particular type of law and a particular type of religion, but also a particular way of

110

thinking. What is beginning is not only a new concept of the dialectical synthesis of law and religion—of justice and grace—but a new concept of synthesis itself, a repudiation of traditional dualistic presuppositions about how men relate to reality. These presuppositions have dominated not only Western legal and religious thought during the past nine centuries but other types of Western thought as well.

Western dualistic thought had its first great impulse in medieval theology, and especially in the famous slogan of St. Anselm, uttered at the end of the eleventh century, *credo ut intelligam*, "I believe in order that I may know." It had its renewal in modern science, and especially in the famous slogan of Descartes in the seventeenth century, *cogito ergo sum*, "I think, therefore I am." The nine-hundred-year-old era that is dying is the era of "I know" and "I think"—the era of the ego, the "I," as a mind that stands outside the objective reality it perceives, the era that has treated first God himself, then nature, and ultimately society, as an external reality to be perceived by the knowing, thinking mind. This is the era of the radical separation of subject from object, of essence from existence, of person from act, of spiritual from secular, of religion from law. Indeed, the dualistic character of traditional Western thought has penetrated almost every kind of analysis. We still debate which is primary, intellect or emotion, ideology or power, the individual or society. In legal analysis we are only very slowly overcoming the dualism of logic versus policy—

a dualism that does injustice to both. Our thinking has traditionally been in terms of such irreducible antitheses, however much we may have recognized the theoretical possibility of their ultimate harmony.[4]

In the last 125 years Marxism has greatly reinforced this dualistic tendency of Western thought by postulating an objective material "base"—the mode of economic production—upon which is built a social and political "superstructure" of institutions and ideas designed to protect the wealth and power of the ruling class. According to Marx, the ideas people hold are an ideology, as he called it, that is, an unconscious reflection of their material class interests. Only the true scientist, he thought, can pierce this ideological veil and see the objective conditions that underlie the conventional myths about law, religion, and other parts of the superstructure.

The basic fallacy here is to suppose that objective social realities such as "the mode of production" and "class relations of production" exist independently of the thoughts and feelings of those who participate in them. A mass of steel and electricity is not a machine until it is so perceived by men. A bricklayer is not a proletarian if he thinks and acts like a prospective shopkeeper. We make up abstract terms like food and sex for various purposes, but what we live with—or without—are such social realities as bread and marriage, and these are products not only of nature but also of ideas and feelings. The history of the past fifty years, especially, cannot be explained by a philosophy that sharply distin-

112

guishes between an objective material reality considered to be basic and a subjective realm of thought and emotion considered to be secondary. More, perhaps, than ever before man has flown in the face of what he is pleased to call his "environment," and has defied his own "material interests" with myths and illusions.

The Marxist theory of objective reality is ultimately derived from the dualism of Thomistic thought. Even scientific atheism, as Leslie Dewart has shown, is the direct heir of medieval Western theology, which separates existence from essence and thus raises the question, "Does God exist?" To say that God "exists" is to speak as though he were a contingent being, an object of perception.[5] We deny God when we speak *about* him as though he were not present.

Similarly, the classical Marxian theory of law as an instrument of class domination is based on the same metaphysical presuppositions as the scholastic natural-law theory which it attacks: it views law, too, as an object of perception, a product detached both from its producer and its consumer, a body of rules that exist externally to the persons who observe them. One may reach the conclusion that this thing is inherently natural, as Thomas Aquinas did, or as a Marxist one may reach the conclusion that it is inherently arbitrary, but in either case one proceeds from what John Dewey many decades ago called "the spectator theory of knowledge," which imagines man as existing outside the universe that he analyzes.

These metaphysical presuppositions which Marxism shares with traditional Western thought have now lost much of their vitality not only in the West but also in those parts of the world where Marxism has been adopted as the official dogma. Both in the Soviet Union and in China the dualism of consciousness and being, of superstructure and base, of mind and matter, of subject and object, has been confined in practice largely to the explanation of social phenomena in the nonsocialist world; otherwise the emphasis is placed—as it is placed increasingly in all countries—on synthesis. Indeed, Soviet and Chinese ideologists proclaim, like Dostoevsky, the imminent transformation of the state—to be sure, not into the Christian church but into a communion of free, socially conscious, dedicated followers of Lenin.

Everywhere synthesis—the overcoming of dualism—is the key to the new kind of thinking which characterizes the new era that we are entering. "Either-or" gives way to "both-and." Not subject versus object but subject and object interacting. Not consciousness versus being but consciousness and being together. Not intellect versus emotion or reason versus passion but the whole man thinking and feeling. Religion *with* law, faith *and* works. Person *and* act: the law should judge the act, but in order to know what kind of an act it really was the judge should put himself in the place of the person who committed it. The just is sacred or it is not just. The sacred is just or it is not sacred.

For law, synthesis means, in part, a new era of reach-

114

ing out to other disciplines and other professions and other social processes—to sociology and economics and political science, to medicine and business management, to poverty and race and international relations, to literature and art and religion. In American law schools we are perhaps about to enter the new era (or at least to knock on its door) with courses in "law and _____": law and medicine, law and economic development, law and race relations, law and psychiatry, (hopefully) law and religion. For religion, similarly, there is a breaking down of barriers: the parish may be the ghetto or the hippies on the common, and the schools of theology are also beginning to pair religion with other disciplines and social processes. Of course the best teachers and the best practitioners of both law and religion have always conceived their respective disciplines in broad terms as interlocking with other disciplines, other professions, and other social processes. What is new is the extent to which this conception is now becoming recognized as central to an understanding of every discipline, and the extent to which it is beginning to be systematized.

The broadening of the categories of the professional and academic disciplines will not be successful, however, unless there is at the same time a broadening of the character of thought itself, and of the language—the discourse—which makes thought what it is. It is not enough for courts to dramatically expand—as they have done during the past four decades—the range of considerations relevant to the decision of a case, in order to in-

115

terpret the law in terms of its social, economic, and political purposes, if at the same time they continue to contrast policy with logic and to treat the former as essentially arbitrary and the latter as essentially mechanical. A policy decision which is illogical is as offensive as a logical decision which is impolitic. What is needed is a logic of policy which will reach results that are *both* desirable in their consequences *and* consistent, objective, and impartial. It is entirely possible to reach so-called "policy decisions" on the basis of so-called "neutral principles."[6] Such "principled preferences" (in David Cavers' phrase) distinguish judicial statesmanship from arbitrariness, on the one hand, and from a mechanical jurisprudence, on the other. Similarly, it is not enough to bring representatives of different professions and disciplines together—politicians, lawyers, economists, sociologists, architects, and social workers, for example, to plan better housing for the poor—unless they are capable of thinking and speaking in ways that will enable them to cooperate with each other; and that means breaking down their traditional dualistic modes of thought and speech. The lawyer must not simply say, "I'm sorry but you cannot do that because there is a rule prohibiting it"; he must also be able to explain the relationship between the rule he is citing and the whole situation of which it —and not only it, but he and they—are a part. In so doing he may find that the obstacle is not insuperable. This is more than getting around the rule: it is restructuring the situation.

116

To bring the law into relationship with other processes of community life and other branches of knowledge is to cease to understand it as an object of perception and to begin to understand it as an enterprise in which the viewer also participates. Judges, for example, cannot be detached from the cases they hear in the way that a laboratory technician is detached from the chemicals he is using. Inevitably they are involved as persons, if only because the parties (or their representatives) speak to them. This makes them more like—though not entirely like—parents attempting to resolve family problems. The difference is that judges are involved also with the public in ways that parents are not. To recognize the judges' various involvements is to provide a basis for reaching impartial decisions. When the interpreter of the law sees his relationship to it not in subject-object terms but in terms of his own participation in the legal process, then it becomes easier for him to define the scope of the leeway that is permitted to him in making his interpretation. Here American courts have had great difficulty, as they have confronted the dilemma of judicial creativity and judicial self-restraint. Both "activists" and "conservatives" tend to treat legal rules as having an independent, objective existence; the activists would manipulate the rules to achieve desired social results, whereas the conservatives would follow the rules—both often fail to recognize that the process of judging is a dynamic one in which the judge (to quote Zechariah Chafee) makes the

117

rules by finding them and finds the rules by making them.[7]

What is true of the significance of synthesis for law is also true of its significance for religion. Here the new age finds expression in the expansion of links between traditional theological disciplines and the social sciences, between the clergy and other professions, between the churches and other social organizations. Also important steps are being taken toward bringing into relationships of community all branches of the Christian church and indeed all the major world religions. These developments have contributed to a new kind of religious thought. There is much less pride in finding theological formulas that show the capacity of the mind to perceive the external object of its inquiry. Thre is much greater concern with the social context of religious doctrine and its relationship to the community in which it is applicable—both the ecclesiastical community and the political community.

Death and Regeneration

The new era is one of synthesis. Yet synthesis alone will not bring us into the new era. We need to believe in a new era—to enter it, to be renewed.

This means not only personal renewal but also, and above all, social renewal, the regeneration of society. It means also something more than mere change. Renewal, regeneration, is a special kind of change which is always accompanied by a special kind of attitude or orientation,

118

and particularly a special kind of orientation toward time, toward history.

Our modern concept of time rests on the religious foundations of Judaism and Christianity. In contrast to the other ancient Indo-European peoples, whose concept of time was cyclical and unhistorical, the Hebrew people developed the concept that time is continuous, irreversible, and historical, leading to ultimate redemption at the end. Nevertheless, Judaic-Christian time also has periods within it. It is not cyclical, but it may be interrupted or accelerated. It develops. Christianity, however, added the new concept of transformation. The Old Testament was transformed in the New. Christ transformed death into a new beginning. Redemption, conversion, not only interrupts history but renews it, regenerates it. "Behold, I make all things new," said Jesus. This introduced a new structure of history, in which there is periodicity, that is, a transformation of one age into another.[8]

The Christian concept of renewal is based on the belief that the end of the world is at hand. To quote Norman O. Brown, this is "not a question of a temporal interval, short or long, but of a visionary breakthrough."

"The Christian sense of history is the sense of living in the last days. Little children, it is the last hour. The whole Christian era is in the last days." "The Christian prayer is for the end of the world: that it may come quickly. The aim is to bring this world to an end; the only question is how. A mistake here might prove quite costly."[9]

119

Eugen Rosenstock-Huessy has shown how the belief in an end-time, the end of the world, the Last Judgment, has influenced the Great Revolutions of Western history. Each of those revolutions translated the experience of death and regeneration into a different concept of the nation and of the church.[10] And when Christian eschatology was discarded by the Enlightenment and by liberal theology in the late eighteenth and nineteenth centuries, a secular eschatology took its place. "No people," he writes, "can live without faith in the ultimate victory of something. So while theology slept, the laity betook itself to other sources of Last Things"—to the eschatology of Karl Marx and of Friedrich Nietzsche.[11]

The belief in and commitment to the possibility and the desirability of entering into a new period of history is a prerequisite to entering into a new period of history. And only in a new period of history, a new era, can there be a renewal, a regeneration, of the whole society, including its religion and its law.

The spiritual death and regeneration of a society, like that of a person, is more than a drastic reform of ideas and conduct; it is more than a drastic reform of ideology and politics. It goes beyond systems of belief and systems of order and justice—it goes beyond religion and beyond law. A society that undergoes such an experience admits that the conditions of its life are intolerable, accepts the bankruptcy of its past, dies to itself; but then it rises above its past, proclaims a new heaven and a new earth, and proceeds to try to live out its new beliefs. Of course,

in one sense this is a religious experience—and in one sense it is a legal experience as well. But it does not come primarily from religion or law; it comes after rejection of the old religion and the old law and before creation of a new religion and a new law. It is the kind of "awakening" that Buddha experienced, when he broke with the past and set out on his Great Going Forth to find Nirvana. It is Christ on the cross reciting the opening words of the twenty-second psalm, which starts with Godforsaken despair and ends with the messianic vision of a redeemed world. Not only individual persons but communities and whole societies may experience such despair and awakening, death and resurrection. This was the experience of the Western Church in 1075 and 1517, and of England, France, and Russia in 1641, 1789, and 1917. Each of these Great Revolutions was more than a reform of political and religious life—not only because it was violent and not only because it changed the power structure of the society but also, and primarily, because it was a collective psychological experience of death and regeneration.

Today the whole of mankind is living through such a revolution. We are experiencing an end-time. Quite literally, two world wars and the threat of a third have put in issue the physical survival of the human race. On another level, Western man has come to the end of an era; he knows that he can no longer dominate the world, but more than that he profoundly questions his past, and he is wholly unsure of his future. On still a

121

third level, within Western civilization, and within other civilizations as well, communities are disintegrating because of racial and religious conflicts, conflicts between the generations, conflicts between the sexes, conflicts between man and the machine technology which he has created, conflicts within each man himself. Of course each of these types of conflict has its own causes; but behind them all stands a deeper cause, namely, the loss of a sense of community, the loss of the capacity to make community; and that, too, is an experience of death.

At the same time there are signs of regeneration. One is the gradual and painful emergence of mankind itself as a community. Another is the widespread formation of local intentional communities, short-lived but intense in their experience of renewal.

The "Communification" of Mankind

For the first time in history, mankind is united in a practical sense. It is united by its capacity to destroy itself. It is united by communications systems that bring every part of the world in almost immediate contact with every other part. It is united by worldwide science and technology, by worldwide trade, by a worldwide system of diplomacy. It shares some features of a common culture. It has the rudiments of a common law.

The idea of the unity of mankind is, of course, not new: it is implicit in the biblical story of creation, and it found its greatest expression in the lives of the great

Hebrew prophets, in Jesus Christ, who died for all men, in St. Paul, who taught that God made of one blood all nations of the earth, and in the lives and teachings of such great personalities as Buddha and Lao-Tzu. What is new is the manifestation of this idea in the gradual emergence of world institutions of a political, economic, and cultural character. These institutions are being forged in the midst of wars which continue to be, for the most part, international in form but which in substance are civil wars, revolutionary wars, precisely because they are being fought within the community of a mankind that is seeking to create for itself a common process of establishing order and justice and a common system of ultimate values.

Mankind already has, of course, the rudiments of a law of international relations, including the law of diplomacy, the law of treaties, the law of international organizations, the law of international trade and finance, the law of conflicts of laws, and other branches of public and private international law. Originally derived from the Western legal tradition, modern international law is now developed by all countries of the world. It is true that states violate international law when they believe it is in their overriding interest to do so; nevertheless, it is important to recognize that without a common legal language the major powers might well have been at full-scale war with each other at any time during the past twenty-five years. Moreover, the fact that governments, groups, and individual persons from all different

123

countries of the world speak with each other in terms of internationally accepted legal norms—negotiate, settle disputes, and jointly regulate their affairs—unquestionably reflects a common legal consciousness and also strengthens, renews, and indeed helps to create that consciousness.

Yet the community of mankind needs much more law. It needs arms reduction agreements. It needs a willingness on the part of the wealthy countries of the world to finance, through the United Nations, substantial economic development among the poor countries. It needs a willingness on the part of the great powers to submit their disputes to impartial adjudication. It needs the expansion of treaty relations, especially of an economic character, between the countries of Western Europe and the United States, on the one hand, and the countries of Eastern Europe and the Soviet Union on the other. Also much remains to be done to bring Communist China into full participation in the international legal community. These and other measures must be taken to strengthen international law if the community of mankind is not to dissolve into anarchy.

If the common law of mankind is rudimentary, its common religion is almost nonexistent. Indeed, it is precisely in its fundamental beliefs that mankind is most divided. Of course, just as a common religion or ideology does not guarantee peace, so religious or ideological differences are not necessarily divisive, provided that a basic humanism and tolerance and respect for law are main-

tained. Yet the lack of a common religious, racial, and cultural consensus among the peoples of the world places a substantial burden on the unifying role of law—as is shown by the experience of the United States, where we have had to rely very heavily on our faith in the Constitution and the courts to unite us just because of our religious, racial, and cultural diversity.

Looking at the world as a whole, it seems apparent that humanism and good will and respect for law cannot alone overcome the gods of Nation and Race and Class, and that some elements of a common universal religion are necessary to give mankind a sense of direction and the courage to face the future. The world needs a radical vision of a common destiny, and common convictions for which people of different nations, races, and classes are willing to make sacrifices; and it needs common rituals and traditions that embody its vision and its convictions.

And so mankind lives on its planet, like the two men under a tree waiting for Godot in Beckett's play—with means of communication but little to say, with some rules to go by but with no assurance they will be followed. Yet it *is* mankind, planetary man—a new creature. The new law that he needs will come—if at all —from a reconstituting of preexisting concepts and processes, "a universalizing and intensifying of them until they are reborn." [12] The new religion will come—if at all—from the prophets, saints, and heroes of the new era.

125

Communes

A second sign of the new era into which we are entering is the widespread formation of temporary local intentional communities, or communes, several thousand of which sprang up in America during the latter half of the 1960s alone. Whatever may be the future of this movement—whose roots lie deep in the past [13]—it is significant because it dramatizes a pervasive quality of life in our time: not only in communes but also in ordinary social experience people seek an outlet for their communal needs in short-lived, intense associations. The commune therefore is a dramatic model for many of the other face-to-face groups of which we are members: neighborhood, school, college, political association, congregation, club, factory, office—and now one must add: encounter group, protest march, and the like.

In all these groups Americans are transients, if only because we move our residences every five years, on the average. Even the family is increasingly made up of transients because of widespread divorce and also because of early departure of children. This is not only an American phenomenon, although America is the extreme example. Family disorganization, labor turnover, and the pressure to move are widespread in most industrial societies. Everywhere, more and more people live in one place, work in another, and take their recreation in a third. Everywhere, more and more rapid and continuous change results in an increasing psychological incapacity

126

to absorb and assimilate it—"future shock," as it has appropriately been called.

Communes respond to this fragmentation of times and spaces not by attempting to impose order on the chaos of life but by carving out some order within a portion of it, temporarily, which makes the rest of it more acceptable. They attempt to concentrate the whole of this transient world for a moment, so to speak, in a single group. The members, mostly young people, usually do not—as their parents do—attempt to preserve some surviving remnants of the old tradition. Instead they generally consider the old to be dead, and they seek regeneration through a wholly new life which, like the society of which it is a part, is transient; indeed, they capitalize on transience. It is the intensity of the local communal experience, coupled with its temporality, the freedom to join or leave, that give it its regenerative power.[14]

This is, in one sense, a "new tribalism," "the global village," as Marshall McLuhan puts it. But the old tribe or old village was permanent and membership was from birth to death and from generation to generation. In Europe fifteen centuries ago the church attacked tribal and village ideology by offering an alternative realm of permanence: the monk died to the world, took a new name, became a new person—forever. Marriage is—was—such a renewal or rebirth into a new life—forever. The concept of "forever" was also translated into secular relationships: the feudal relationship of lord and vassal, the modern landed estate that remained in the same

127

family for generations or even centuries, the business or handicraft handed down from father to son, were secular approximations of immortality. In the past fifty years, in the past thirty years, most of our immortality has disappeared. We now take our communities on the run.

In terms of law and religion, the situation of the communes makes a sharp contrast with that of mankind. Mankind has a rudimentary legal system and diverse religions. The commune usually has a rudimentary religion and almost no common law. Its religion is usually expressed in its sense of joy, wonder, love, beauty, sanctity. But it also has need of some kind of informal customary law to keep peace among its members and to operate efficiently as well as to protect itself against hostile forces outside it. (For example, leaders of some communes have adopted all the other members in order that they might become a "family" within the zoning requirements of the localities where they are situated.) Of course, the members bring with them from the outside world some concepts of the binding force of agreements, marriage obligations, responsibility for children, due care, causation, individual and group property, and the like; and they anticipate returning to the outside world at some future time. Still, many communes suffer badly from lack of norms and procedures for reaching agreements, resolving conflicts, and channeling cooperation.

The regenerative experience of the commune is the total immersion of its members in a group; for a time;

in response to death, suffering, war, oppression, birth, love, service; with a sense that the traditions of the past are exhausted and that society is doomed; but also with a sense of affirmation and renewal. Many would call this a religious experience, but it is beyond religion in the usual sense of a system of beliefs and of worship. It is the experience of death and rebirth that may come to a man or to a community, regardless of his or its religion or ideology, at a time of disillusionment, despair, and apathy.

Those who undergo such an experience have something to tell the rest of society. In particular, they have something to tell us about the revitalization of the local communities in which we live: the family, the neighborhood, the school, the college, the congregation, the factory, the office. This, in turn, may tell us something important about the revitalization of our cities and of the nation and of mankind. One part of the message will surely have to do with the interaction of religion and law. Another will have to do with synthesis and regeneration.

We return to "Alyosha out in the world." How are inner experiences of holiness and faith to be translated into social structures and processes for allocating rights and duties—and vice-versa? How are order and justice to be internalized in the conscience of every person?

Ivan Karamazov contends that social institutions, by their very nature, must sacrifice persons for statistics,

129

the unique for the general, while true Christianity, being concerned with the free human soul, necessarily sacrifices the general for the unique. But this dualism is intolerable for Ivan. How, he asks, can one accept a God who, in the name of spiritual freedom, permits men to practice injustice and suffering—above all, bestial cruelty to little children? Ivan's answer is to give God back the ticket to life. Alyosha's answer is the saintly Father Zossima: it is, in other words, a rejection of the question. For Father Zossima, as for the Russian Orthodox Church, the only hope is the communion of saints, the togetherness of the faithful. In a hostile world, the church must accept the role of the suffering servant, despised and rejected, and must bear witness to the truth through worship and the sacraments and a life of Christian humility and love.

For Western Christianity, both Catholic and Protestant, Eastern Orthodoxy has seemed too mystical and otherworldly. In the West, the church has traditionally considered it to be one of the main tasks of Christianity to help reform social institutions—not merely by prayer and not merely by example but by active social and political measures. When organized religion in the West has abdicated its social and political responsibilities, secular organizations have arisen to pour religious zeal into programs of law reform.

Neither the personal mysticism of the East nor the social activism of the West seems to hold the key to the interrelationship of religion and law in our time.

The former comes too close to religiosity, the latter too close to legalism.

The hope is in a new era of synthesis; the hope is that as a people, as a civilization, and as mankind, we may have the patience to suffer the death of the old era and the inspiration to be regenerated.

● Postscript

This postscript is written for those who would wish that more had been said in these chapters about the tensions between law and religion and who may be concerned lest in celebrating, so to speak, their intermarriage we may only succed in sanctifying the one and petrifying the other.

The tensions between law and religion are most apparent in those Eastern cultures whose religion is essentially mystical and personal, and whose official legal structures—perhaps partly for that very reason—tend to be excessively formalistic and mechanical. But even in cultures whose religion is essentially legal and social, like the Hebrew and the Muslim, there are tensions between the prophetic and the priestly aspects of the culture as well as between the mystical and the rational aspects. And perhaps more than any other religion, Christianity, with its intense combination of mystical

133

and legal elements, has been obsessed with the paradoxes of grace and justice.

In contemporary Western thought those paradoxes have been reduced to commonplace formulas widely accepted as axiomatic. Law, we are accustomed to say, deals with the normal situation, with general categories of persons, with "the greatest good for the greatest number"; religion, on the other hand, is concerned with a man's unique personality, his need for moral standards that transcend social utility, his need to understand the meaning of life and to cope with death. Thus we think of law primarily as a matter of social action and of religion primarily as a matter of personal psychology —"what the individual does with his own solitariness," in Whitehead's phrase. Law may say, your country needs you to fight for it; religion may say, my faith forbids me to. Law may say, it is a crime to take the life of a sick man; religion may say, there are no rules applicable to a unique situation—one must do what love requires.

This is not merely a conflict between law and morality or society and conscience. The tension lies much deeper. It is a tension between morality, whether social or personal, and man's sense of wonder and grace, his sense of contact with other worlds, his sense of belonging. Social justice, equality, due process of law—and also personal honesty, decency, love of neighbor—enormously desirable as they are, will not necessarily create the mystery and beauty and sense of ultimate purpose with-

out which life is impoverished. One need not adhere to the radical left to appreciate its concern that the new structures of society introduced by orthodox revolutionaries, no matter how much more just than the structures which they replace, may nevertheless only perpetuate man's alienation. And so religion challenges law not only on the level of duty but also, and primarily, on the level of aspiration.

The other side of the tension is the need to preserve law from interference by religious considerations that are irrelevant and possibly harmful. Law, after all, whatever else it may also be, is a highly complex and intricate system of processes and techniques for making, interpeting, and applying rules. The system is not necessarily aided, and is likely to be substantially hurt, by a preoccupation with questions of personal morality, let alone spirituality. It is true that normally the policies which law is supposed to serve, and the values which are implicit in it, should be consistent with policies and values proclaimed by religion. The usual formula is that law is ultimately based on morality and morality is ultimately based on religion.[1] But the ways in which law mediates policies and values in individual situations must, above all, be consistent with each other, for it is, above all, that internal consistency which testifies to the generality and objectivity of law which are, in turn, its fundamental qualities. These qualities of generality and objectivity challenge the personal moral and spiritual values commonly associated with religion. Should the

135

jury be allowed to hear evidence that the plaintiff is poor and the defendant is rich, or vice versa? Should a judge refuse to grant a divorce because his religion teaches that whom God hath joined together no man should put asunder? Law challenges religion on the level of equality and dispassionateness.

The tensions between law and religion help to preserve each from swallowing up the other. Religion, by standing outside the law, helps to prevent it from becoming deified; prophetic religion—and its offspring, prophetic ideology—are necessary safeguards against a Caesaro-Papism which would demand that the existing legal order be not merely respected but also worshiped. Conversely, law, by its secularity and by its withdrawal from religion, leaves religion free to develop in its own way, and thus helps it to avoid legalization and ultimately petrification; so long as the regulation of social life is seen to be within the province of the state alone, the church can avoid the temptation of being transformed into a political organization, and at the same time its practices and creeds, lacking legal institutionalization, are in less danger of becoming objects of idolatry.

Finally, the tension between religion and law are presupposed in our constitutional doctrine of separation of church and state—a doctrine which is, on the one hand, the cornerstone of the religious liberties of minorities and, on the other, an essential protection of the political power of the majority.

We do not deny the importance of maintaining these

tensions between law and religion when we affirm, nevertheless, that there are religious dimensions of law and legal dimensions of religion, and that the two cannot survive independently of each other. Indeed, the tensions between the two are also tensions within each—between its structural and its spiritual aspects: within law, the tensions between justice and mercy, between the general rule and its application in the exceptional case, as well as the tensions between the rational, utilitarian aspects of law and its more mysterious aspects of ritual, tradition, authority, and universality; within religion, the tensions between ecclesiastical institutions and the freedom of the spirit to move where it pleases, between organized religion and the preaching of the Word.

Yet when we have said all this, we nevertheless come to the point where these tensions, though necessary and valuable to maintain, must somehow be resolved or they will destroy us. It is that point from which this book takes off. A healthy legal system must combine rule and discretion, strict law and equity. A healthy religious system must combine priestly and prophetic functions. A healthy society must combine a healthy legal order and a healthy religious faith. There must be a synthesis of these opposing elements.

The dialectical unity of law and religion as dimensions of social experience does not exclude the separation of particular legal and religious institutions. It only requires a recognition of their ultimate interaction. At the highest

137

level, surely, the just and the holy are one—or else not only all men but the whole universe, and God himself, are condemned to an eternal schizophrenia. It is necessary to say this because the conventional wisdom has separated these two aspects of life to the point of disaster. Only after we have grasped the interdependence of law and religion as two opposite but reconcilable dimensions of experience are we in a position to face the delicate balance between the secular and the sacred aspects of particular existing social institutions.

Moreover, in attempting to restate the proper relationship between law and religion, it is important to recognize that the crisis which confronts Western man today—as contrasted with earlier times—is not the danger of excessive sanctification of law or excessive legalization of religion; it is not a crisis of their excessive integration but rather a crisis of their excessive fragmentation. In the United States of America, certainly, we are threatened more by contempt for law than by worship of it, and more by an overwhelming skepticism regarding the future than by some great all-embracing totalitarian eschatology. In some other periods of history, and in some other parts of the world today, an emphasis on the tensions between law and religion, or between structural and spiritual values, may be fully justified. Especially where a state attempts to impose a particular system of belief on its people, it is important to oppose such a usurpation of religious authority by political leaders, and

138

to reassert the inherent right of individuals and of groups to maintain their own spiritual values, their own belief systems. Also where a church attempts to impose its political views on a society, claiming divine sanction for them, it is necessary to oppose such a usurpation of secular authority by religious leaders, and to reassert the independence of the state. The dualism of church and state, spiritual and secular, religion and law, makes sense as an answer to monistic claims of the total state or of the total church. In the United States today, however, and in most countries of Western Europe, the principal danger is not that of excessive spiritual claims by political parties or excessive political claims by religious or quasi-religious groups. We are threatened more by anarchy than by dictatorship, and more by decadence and apathy than by fanaticism. Under these circumstances, the old dualisms need to be subordinated to a more complex unity, which seeks the interaction of secular and spiritual aspects of life rather than their compartmentalization.

The practical danger of any organic theory of society is that it may be used irresponsibly to sanctify and petrify the particular existing laws and the particular existing orthodoxies of a given social order. This danger is particularly acute when law and religion do not carry within themselves built-in principles of change. The danger is much less acute in a society such as our own, where religious traditions are founded on the concept

139

of change. Indeed, in the Western tradition it is a fundamental purpose of religion to challenge law to change continually in order to be more humane, and a fundamental purpose of law to challenge religion to change continually in order to be more socially responsible. An organic theory of society does not protect the status quo when the theory itself conceives the society in terms of a dynamic process of development.

In America the dynamic character both of law and of religion—the capacity of each to change, to develop, and even to die and be regenerated—makes it possible for them to support each other without overstepping the constitutional boundaries that separate them. The people who framed the First Amendment of the Constitution almost certainly would have agreed with the view expressed in this book that law, the Constitution itself, could not survive the disappearance of religious faith in this country. It was partly for that reason (and not only to protect civil liberties) that they forbade the enacting of any law prohibiting "the free exercise" of religion. At the same time, they were concerned lest the government should prefer one set of religious beliefs or practices over another or, for that matter, religious beliefs over irreligious beliefs; and so, by the clause forbidding any "establishment" of religion, they prohibited government aid to religion—not all kinds of government aid, but those kinds which could be considered an "establishment." Over the decades, and especially in the last thirty years, the Supreme Court of the United

States has declared many forms of government aid to religion to be invalid under the "establishment" clause. Yet it is clear that the legislature may take some measures to protect the free exercise of religion without necessarily effecting an establishment. For example, it may permit religious organizations to be exempt from taxation; it may permit contributions to religious causes to be deducted from taxable income; it may permit chaplains to be employed by the armed forces; it may exempt from military service persons who object to such service on religious grounds; it may give some kinds of indirect support to parochial schools; it may provide programs of released time or shared time in public schools to enable pupils to have religious instruction elsewhere; it may not provide for religious instruction or the saying of prayers as part of public school exercises, but it may provide for instruction about religion—courses in religious history, religious philosophy, religious literature, and the like. The view that law needs religion for its inspiration does not imply that responsibility for the encouragement of religion should be shifted from the people—where it belongs—to the government or to the legal system; it only implies that the government, by law, should cooperate to the extent of its constitutional powers in providing an environment in which religion may flourish.

False religion as well as true religion? Yes. Secular religions? Atheistic religions? Certainly. For all of them ask the fundamental questions—what Dostoevsky

called the "cursed questions"—that have to be asked if our society is to find its integrity. All of them cultivate the religious dimensions of social experience which, together with the legal dimensions, integrate the times and spaces in which we live.

● Notes

Chapter I

1. The phrase "integrity crisis" is derived from the writings of
   Eric Erikson; it is less well known than his phrase "identity
   crisis," perhaps because the latter phrase relates to the transition from youth to adulthood, which is open and notorious,
   whereas the former relates to the "closure" of the whole life
   cycle, about which there is apt to be more secrecy and more
   embarrassment. Erikson speaks of "the despair of the knowledge that a limited life is coming to a conscious conclusion."
   He describes in the following terms the integrity needed to
   balance such despair: "It is the ego's accrued assurance of
   its proclivity for order and meaning. It is a post-narcissistic
   love of the human ego—not of the self—as an experience
   which conveys some world order and spiritual sense, no
   matter how dearly paid for. It is the acceptance of one's
   one and only life cycle as something that had to be and
   that, by necessity, permitted of no substitutions: it thus
   means a new and a different love of one's parents. It is a
   comradeship with the ordering ways of distant times and
   different pursuits, as expressed in the simple products and
   sayings of such times and pursuits. Although aware of the
   relativity of all the various life styles which have given

meaning to human striving, the possessor of integrity is ready to defend the dignity of his own life style against all physical and economic threats. For he knows that an individual life is the accidental coincidence of but one life cycle with but one segment of history; and that for him all human integrity stands or falls with the one style of integrity of which he partakes. The style of integrity developed by his culture or civilization thus becomes the 'patrimony of his soul.' . . . Before this final solution, death loses its sting." Erikson, *Childhood and Society* (2nd. ed., New York, 1963), p. 268, *Insight and Responsibility* (New York, 1964), p. 134. This is not the place to develop the idea—we shall return to it in chapter IV—that whole societies may undergo stages of development analogous to stages in the life cycle of an individual person.

2. *Childhood and Society,* p. 268.

3. Cf. Eugen Rosenstock-Huessy, *Speech and Reality* (Norwich, Vt., 1970), pp. 12 ff. Some readers may at this point want more precise definitions of law and religion. The author begs their indulgence: in a sense, the four chapters as a whole are a search for the right definitions of these two terms. However, it may be helpful at the outset to emphasize several points in explanation of this paragraph. First, we view law not only as a social but also as a psychological phenomenon: it involves the sense of social order, the sense of rights and duties, the sense of the just, which is felt by individual members of society, and not only the society's collective system of regulation. Second, we view religion not only as a psychological phenomenon but also as a social phenomenon: it involves a society's collective concern with transcendent values, and not only the individual's personal beliefs. Both law and religion are thus to be seen as dimensions both of human nature and of social relations. Third, we avoid the question whether religion necessarily involves a belief in a divine being or beings. Instead, we treat as religion those sets of beliefs and practices which give to any persons or things or forces—whether or not they are expressly considered divine—the same kinds of devotion and attribute to them the same

kinds of powers that are usually given and attributed to God or to gods in conventional deistic religions. For example, Soviet schoolchildren are taught to say: "Lenin lived. Lenin lives. Lenin will live." This we would call an expression of a religious faith, even though the same Soviet schoolchildren are taught to be atheists and antireligious.

The statement that religion "is people manifesting a collective concern for the ultimate meaning and purpose of life—it is a shared intuition of, and commitment to, transcendent values" is not intended as a comprehensive definition of religion but rather as an indication of its central aspects. There are other aspects, such as the inner life of the solitary mystic, but I believe that these are ultimately dependent on the collective faith. Also it is possible to find contrasts and tensions between "ultimate" and "transcendent," between "meaning" and "values," and between "concern" and "intuition" or "commitment"; yet for present purposes I believe that these terms should be seen as complementary rather than contradictory to each other. Readers who wish to grapple further with problems of definition of the scope of the concept of religion may consult such recent works as Rem B. Edwards, *Reason and Religion: An Introduction to the Philosophy of Religion* (New York, 1972), Roland Robertson, *The Sociological Interpretation of Religion* (Oxford, 1970), and Peter L. Berger, *The Sacred Canopy: Elements of a Sociological Theory of Religion* (New York, 1967). Of these, the last is closest to my way of thinking, especially in that it avoids the tendency of many to reduce religion to metaphysics or to morals or to both (cf. Geertz, "Religion: An Anthropological Study," in *Encyclopedia of the Social Sciences*, pp. 400, 406).

4. Cf. Huston Smith, *The Religions of Man* (New York, 1958), pp. 90-92, where ritual, tradition, and authority are listed among six aspects of religion which "appear so regularly as to suggest that their need is rooted in man's very makeup to an extent that no religion which proposes to speak to mankind at large can expect to elude them indefinitely." A fourth element listed by Smith is "the concept of God's

sovereignty and grace"; for this we have substituted the concept of universality, since we include among religions world faiths that purport not to recognize the existence of God. Smith's other two aspects of all world religions are speculation (in the sense of metaphysical wondering) and mystery (in the sense of the occult and the uncanny).

See also Roscoe Pound, *Law and Religion* (Rice Institute Pamphlet, XXVII, April, 1940), where authority and universality are treated as ideas which religion has contributed to law. However, Pound treats religion as one of the competing sources of the received ideals of a given legal system rather than as a necessary dimension of law.

Most anthropological studies dealing with the relation of law to religion in primitive societies define religion too narrowly for our purposes, confining its meaning to supernaturalism and magic.

5. See Max Weber, *On Law in Economy and Society,* Max Rheinstein, ed. (Cambridge, Mass., 1954), pp. 224-83. A widely used contemporary textbook in sociology, influenced by Weber, contains the following discussion of secularism and rationality: "Modern man feels freer to ask, 'What good is it?' The world has become 'disenchanted,' more 'sensate,' more 'materialistic,' less 'spiritual,' to use terms that have been applied to this trend toward *secularism*. Secularism encourages *rationality* in social organization. Group ways of acting are consciously designed and measured by effectiveness and efficiency. . . . Secularism and rationality are associated with *impersonality* in human relations. With a weakened sense of kinship and with a utilitarian orientation, it is easy to treat people as means rather than as ends." Leonard Broom and Philip Selznick, *Sociology: A Text with Adapted Readings,* (4th ed., New York, 1968), pp. 47-48.

6. Thomas M. Franck, *The Structure of Impartiality: Examining the Riddle of One Law in a Fragmented World* (New York, 1968), pp. 62, 68-69.

7. The Swiss psychologist Jean Piaget pioneered studies of the moral development of children showing the importance of

146

cognitive, as contrasted with coercive, factors. Cf. Piaget, *The Moral Judgment of the Child* (New York, 1932). More recently Lawrence Kohlberg has built on Piaget's work, demonstrating the universality of sequential modes of thought about rights, obedience, justice. Cf. L. Kohlberg and E. Turiel, eds., *Research in Moralization: The Cognitive-Developmental Approach* (New York, 1972). See also Derek Wright, *The Psychology of Moral Behavior* (Baltimore, 1971). Cross-cultural psychological studies by June L. Tapp, influenced by the theories of Piaget and Kohlberg, emphasize the importance of the factors listed in the text—affiliation, credibility, fairness, and trust—in children's development of principles for evaluating right and wrong and for perfecting a sense of law and justice. Cf. June L. Tapp and F. J. Levine, "Persuasion to Virtue: A Preliminary Statement," *Law and Society Review* IV (1970), 565, 576-81; June L. Tapp, ed., "Socialization, the Law, and Society," *Journal of Social Issues* XXVII (1971). Erik Erikson, in his essay "Identity and the Life Cycle," *Psychological Issues* I (1959) discusses the importance of trust and affiliation in developing notions of law and justice; later works of Erikson also stress these factors. Cf. his *Insight and Responsibility* (New York, 1964).

8. See Harold J. Berman, *Justice in the U.S.S.R.: An Interpretation of Soviet Law* (2nd ed., Cambridge, Mass., 1963), pp. 46-65. Initially it had been the official Soviet theory that in a proletarian dictatorship law is a temporary expedient, essentially "bourgeois" in nature, needed to maintain state power in the transition from capitalism to socialism but ultimately destined to die out under socialism. In the mid-1930s this theory was denounced as an expression of "legal nihilism," and instead it was proclaimed that under socialism law expresses the will of the whole people and as such commands not only obedience and rational assent but also loyalty and faith. The idea that socialist law is sacred was not contradicted —in Stalin's mind—by the use of terror against enemies (or, indeed, potential enemies); on the contrary, it was the very sanctity of Soviet law that served to justify the ruthless

147

destruction of those whose loyalty to it, or faith in it, was called in question. This, of course, is the great danger in any social system that sanctifies law to the point of wholly identifying it with religion (or with a quasi-religious ideology). We shall have more to say about that danger in the next chapter. In this chapter we are concerned with the opposite danger—the danger not of tyranny but of anarchy—that arises when law is secularized and wholly divorced from religion (or from ideology).

9. Franck, *The Structure of Impartiality*, p. 62.

10. This incident is reported from memory, the author having been a student in Professor-Judge Arnold's class at the time. The same ambivalence toward legal ritual and legal myths is reflected in Arnold's two major works, *The Symbols of Government* (New York, 1935) and *Folklore of Capitalism* (New York, 1937).

11. Among the "moral feelings," or "moral sentiments," John Rawls, following Kant, includes guilt, shame, remorse, indignation, resentment, and the like; he classifies love, friendship, trust, and the like as "natural feelings," or natural attitudes. See Rawls, *A Theory of Justice* (Cambridge, Mass., 1971), pp. 479-90. But surely moral feelings include not only negative but also positive feelings—such as innocence, pride, satisfaction, thankfulness, and others. Also there are feelings of cooperation, sharing, solidarity, and reciprocity, which must be classified as (at least partly) moral. But apart from the Kantian and post-Kantian range of moral and natural feelings there are also legal feelings, such as the feeling of entitlement, the feeling of violation of rights, the feeling of legal obligation, the feeling that like cases should be decided alike, the satisfaction of a fair hearing, and others. A pioneer in the study of such legal emotions was the prerevolutionary Russian-Polish jurist Leon Petrazhitsky; see *Law and Morality: Leon Petrazycki*, trans. Hugh W. Babb, with an introduction by Nicholas S. Timasheff (Cambridge, Mass., 1955).

12. Although there is a burgeoning literature on the role of

celebration and play in social life generally, surprisingly little has been written about their role in the legal process. However, Johan Huizinga's pioneer book, *Homo Ludens: A Study of the Play Element in Culture* (Boston, 1955), contains a short chapter on "Play and Law," focusing chiefly on the elements of contest (*agon*) in trial procedure in archaic law. Huizinga writes: "The winning as such is, for the archaic mind, proof of truth and rightness" (p. 81). The ordeal, the wager, the vow, and various forms of potlatch are among the examples given by Huizinga of the play element in law. He writes: "In Rome, too, any and every means of undoing the other party in a lawsuit was held as licit for a long time. The parties draped themselves in mourning, sighed, sobbed, loudly invoked the common weal, packed the court with witnesses and clients to make the proceedings more impressive. In short, they did everything we do today" (p. 87).

The importance of celebration in social life is reaffirmed in Harvey Cox's *The Feast of Fools: A Theological Essay on Festivity and Fantasy* (Cambridge, Mass., 1969), which, however, unfortunately omits consideration of legal ceremonies, perhaps because it is primarily concerned with less solemn and less structured forms of celebration. However, the distinction between spontaneous festive play (frolic, fantasy, etc.) and structured games—a distinction which some writers have charged Huizinga with failing to make—can easily be overdrawn. The cardinal point is that the game, whether or not structured, is played for its own sake, as an end in itself.

Just as philosophers of ritual have written little about law, so philosophers of law have written little about ritual, except occasionally to discuss its utility, or lack thereof, in facilitating the aims of a legal system. Thus Lon L. Fuller stresses the communicative function of ritual in signaling and clarifying interactional expectancies. See Fuller, "Human Interaction and the Law," *The American Journal of Jurisprudence* XIV (1969), 6 ff. From another point of view, Charles Fried has written of trial procedure as a dramatization of principles of justice. Criminal procedure, in particular, he writes, is "ex-

pressive of [the] relation of trust and respect for the accused, for his victim, and for all potential participants in the criminal process. When the accused is presented as an equal of the accuser, his stature as a member of the community is dramatically affirmed. Moreover, there is dramatically affirmed the community's commitment to the principle of justice as superior to material advantage. In a sense every rational action is a dramatization of its principle; procedure, however, bears a particularly close affinity to drama and to ritual. Legal procedure might well be classed as a moral ritual or a ritual of justice." Fried, *Anatomy of Values: Problems of Personal and Social Choice* (Cambridge, Mass., 1970), pp. 129-32. This comes close to saying that ritual is an essential element of law (or at least of "legal procedure")—part of its basic reality, and not merely a means to other legal ends. Yet the passage also suggests that the basic reality of any legal (or other rational) action is to be found in "its principle," of which the action is a (mere?) dramatization. The point being made in the text is that principle and action are one: in opposition to Platonic concepts, we assert that all legal speech is, in part, a ritual, and that the meaning of the ritual is to be found in itself—in its context—and not in some preexisting idea or principle which it embodies.

13. That time itself is a religious category has been demonstrated in Mircea Eliade's studies of the antithesis between archaic time, which, being based on a religion of periodic redemption, is cyclical and unhistorical, and Judaic-Christian time, which is progressive (historical), continuous, and irreversible, being based on a religion of ultimate redemption at the end. Cf. Eliade, *Cosmos and History: The Myth of the Eternal Return*, trans. Willard R. Trask (New York, 1959). Eliade mentions (pp. 31-32) as "too well known for us to insist upon" the fact that "human justice, which is founded upon the idea of 'law,' has a celestial and transcendent model in the cosmic norms (*tao, artha, rta, tsedek, themis*, etc.)." In archaic or traditional societies (as Eliade calls them), human law is viewed as a repetition of a divine or cosmic justice which

first occurred in mythical time, that is, at the extratemporal instant of the beginning, whereas in the monotheistic revelation of Judaism, Moses received the law at a certain place and at a certain date (cf. p. 105), and it is replenished by interpretation from time to time. In the next chapter and in chapter IV we shall consider the effect of Christian concepts of time on the notion of the continuity, or ongoingness, of law.

14. Cf. Søren Kierkegaard, *Fear and Trembling*, trans. Robert Payne (Oxford, 1939). Rudolf Otto, *The Idea of the Holy*, trans. John W. Harvey (New York, 1958).

15. See chapter II of this book.

16. Reinhold Niebuhr, "Faith as the Sense of Meaning in Human Existence," *Christianity and Crisis* XXVI (June 13, 1966), 127.

17. Recent examples are Lon L. Fuller, *The Morality of Law* (2nd ed., New Haven, Conn., 1963) and Charles Fried, *An Anatomy of Values*. Both these books take it for granted that law may be judged solely by its success or failure in promoting its own ends—namely, justice and order; neither judges law by the extent to which it expresses the values which give a society its sense of its own identity and of its mission. In the closing pages of *The Morality of Law*, Fuller suggests, however, that the morality inherent in law itself cannot define the community to which a given body of law is applicable, and he briefly discusses communication and language as a precondition of legal morality. This would mean that justice depends on something beyond itself. Also in his article "Two Principles of Human Association," *Nomos* XI (1969). Fuller concludes: "May there not be in human nature a deep hunger to form a bond of union with one's fellows which runs deeper than that of legally defined duty and counterduty? . . . Corresponding to the nightmare world of Orwell's in 1984, where Big Brother watches over you to see that you believe right and think right, may there not be a counternightmare in which no one cares what you think or believe . . . ? Has the frigid legal atmosphere of our basic

151

associations driven some of us, in search of a richer bond of union with our fellows, into becoming Mods, or Rockers, or Hell's Angels, and shouters of filthy words? These are difficult questions to which there can be no single big answer. What I am disturbed about is that we are every day, in a multitude of different contexts, giving little answers to them. No doubt most of these little answers are right. Yet in their cumulative effect they may push us along a path which we do not like and would not have entered so blithely had we known where it was taking us" (p. 21). This passage seems to say that the morality inherent in law itself depends on a sense of community which transcends that morality.

18. Christopher Dawson, *Religion and Culture* (New York, 1948), pp. 154-55: "The secularization of law in Greece was like the secularization of philosophy. If they were rationalized, reason itself was divinized, and the lawgiver and the philosopher never entirely lost their sacred and prophetic character." Cf. Eric A. Havelock, *Preface to Plato* (Cambridge, Mass., 1953).

19. It is a cardinal principle of the Western religious tradition (both in its Christian and its Judaic aspects) to "hate the sin but love the sinner." Unfortunately, that principle is often violated—on the one hand by those whose sympathetic concern for the criminal undermines their indignation at the criminal act, and on the other hand by those whose indignation at the criminal act undermines their sympathetic concern for the person who committed it.

The main reason criminal sanctions should be removed from many types of so-called victimless crimes is that the absence of a complainant makes it very difficult to obtain evidence sufficient to convict, and this in turn leads to police abuses in obtaining evidence and to police corruption. The other argument often made—that the offenses in question should not be criminally punishable because they are merely acts of personal immorality—simply assumes that they do not also harm society. In principle, no act should be made criminally punishable unless it is both wrongful (immoral) and harmful to

society (antisocial). Today opinions differ regarding both the moral and the social aspects of homosexuality, but none would deny that the other offenses listed—excessive drinking, drug abuse, prostitution, and gambling—should be subject to some form of public control, which inevitably also means some kind of criminal sanction for violating such control.

Nevertheless, the crimes in question—which we must continually remember constitute the bulk of the crimes committed in the United States in our time and are at the root of organized crime and of police corruption—are significantly different from "crimes against the person" (homicide, rape, assault and battery, etc.) and "crimes against property" (burglary, larceny, embezzlement, etc.). A crime such as gambling or prostitution or drug abuse usually involves no desire to cause harm and no consciousness of moral wrongdoing, but rather a defiance of orthodox community values. It is partly for this reason that it is important to involve a wide circle of people other than law enforcement officials in the treatment of such misconduct. Thus far, however, except for the important role of social workers (in which the United States has been the pioneer and the outstanding example), little has been done to bring about such community involvement. We shall return to this matter in chapter IV.

20. Cf. M. L. Levine, G. C. McNamee, and D. Greenberg, eds., *The Tales of Hoffman* (New York, 1970), an abridgment of the trial of the Chicago seven, with an introduction by Dwight Macdonald.

21. Cf. Daniel Berrigan, *The Trial of the Catonsville Nine* (Boston, 1970).

22. Max Weber, "Science as a Vocation," in H. H. Gerth and C. Wright Mills, trans. and eds., *From Max Weber: Essays in Sociology* (New York, 1958), pp. 155-56. Weber added: "It is not accidental . . . that today only within the smallest and [most] intimate circles, in personal human situations, in *pianissimo,* that something is pulsating that corresponds to the prophetic *pneuma* which in former times swept through the great communities like a firebrand, welding

them together." Although he seemed to deplore this disenchantment, Weber nevertheless rejected any role for the intellectual in attempting to change it other than the role of maintaining "plain intellectual integrity" and of meeting "the demands of the day." Ultimately Hitler took over.

23. *Ibid.*

24. Cf. Robert N. Bellah, "Civil Religion in America," in William G. McLaughlin and Robert N. Bellah, eds. *Religion in America* (Boston, 1968). Bellah traces the idea of civil religion (the phrase itself is Rousseau's) to the Founding Fathers. He writes that "from the earliest years of the republic" we have had "a collection of beliefs, symbols, and rituals with respect to sacred things and institutionalized in a collectivity. This religion—there seems no other word for it—while not antithetical to and indeed sharing much in common with Christianity, was neither sectarian nor in any specific sense Christian"—though at first the society itself "was overwhelmingly Christian" (p. 10). "Behind the civil religion at every point lie Biblical archetypes: Exodus, Chosen People, Promised Land, New Jerusalem, Sacrificial Death and Rebirth. But it is also genuinely American and genuinely new. It has its own prophets and its own martyrs, its own sacred events and sacred places, its own solemn rituals and symbols. It is concerned that America be a society as perfectly in accord with the will of God as men can make it, and a light to all the nations" (p. 20).

Chapter II

1. See Martin Buber, *Between Man and Man,* trans. R. G. Smith (Boston, 1955), p. 128.

2. José Ortega y Gasset, *Toward a Philosophy of History* (New York, 1941), p. 217.

3. The belief in socialism, like the belief in democracy has, to be sure, lost some of its religious fervor in the latter half of the twentieth century, as the sense of its apocalyptic mission has declined. That socialism nevertheless remains an

"ism," a matter of faith—not only in China, but also in the Soviet Union—is illustrated by the following story told by an American observer of Soviet education: "The four-year-old daughter of an Asian diplomat [in Moscow] was attending a Russian kindergarten. She came home one day and stared with unusual concentration at a small statue of Buddha in the corner of the living room. 'What does Buddha mean?' she asked her mother. 'Buddha is not exactly a god,' her mother replied, 'although he is something like what your friends from other countries call God. We consider him the wisest of teachers, someone who has shown us how to live.' The child answered, 'But Lenin is our only God.' The exchange illustrates an important difference between the patriotic propaganda directed at small children in the Soviet Union and comparable efforts in the United States. American youngsters are taught to honor historical figures like George Washington and Abraham Lincoln. Soviet children are expected to love Lenin. In a very real sense, the patriotic training children receive in Soviet kindergartens is comparable to religious education in other countries." Susan Jacoby, "Who Raises Russia's Children?" *The Saturday Review,* August 21, 1971, p. 53.

4. See note 15 of this chapter and accompanying text.

5. See the Preamble of the *Ecloga* (a collection of laws promulgated by the Byzantine emperors in about A.D. 740), Edwin H. Freshfield, *A Manual of Roman Law, the Ecloga* (Cambridge, Mass., 1926). The opening paragaph states: "A selection of laws arranged in compendious form by Leo and Constantine, the wise and pious Emperors, taken from the Institutes, the Digests, the Code, and the Novels of the Great Justinian, and revised in the direction of greater humanity, promulgated in the month of March, Ninth Indiction in the year of the world 6234." It goes on:

"In the name of the Father and the Son and of the Holy Ghost, Leo and Constantine, faithful Emperors of the Romans.

"Our God, the master and maker of all things, created man and honored him with the privilege of free will, and gave him

155

a law in the words of the prophecy to help him and thereby make known to him all things which he should do and should not do, so that he might choose the former as hosts of salvation and eschew the latter as the causes of punishment.

"And we do exhort all those who have been appointed to administer the law and enjoin them to abstain from all human passions and by a sound understanding to pronounce the sentences of true justice, neither despising the poor nor permitting a powerful transgressor to go unpunished, nor in appearance and work to set justice and equity on a pedestal but in reality choosing injustice and cupidity as profitable. But when two persons have a suit before them, the one having become rich and the other poor, to make equity between them, taking from the former the amount of which the latter has been unjustly deprived. For there are some who do not treasure truth and justice in their hearts but, corrupted by riches, willing to favor for friendship's sake, revengeful through personal enmity, importunate in office are incapable of doing justice and illustrate in their lives the true work of the psalmist, 'Do ye indeed speak righteousness, do ye indeed judge rightly, ye sons of men? For indeed ye work wickedness in your hearts on earth, your hands wreak injustice.' [Psalms 58:1-2.]

"Let those who are appointed by our pious Majesty to try cases and decide disputes and who are entrusted with the true scales of our august laws reflect upon these matters, let them take them to heart. Our Lord, Jesus Christ, hath said, 'Judge not according to appearance but judge a righteous judgment' [John 7:24], a judgment free from all favor of reward. For it stands written, 'Woe to those judging unrighteously for the sake of rewards, who turn aside the way of the meek and take away the just due of the righteous from him; their root shall be as dust and their blossom shall go up as dust because they wished not to fulfill the law of the Lord' [Amos 2:6, 7].

"For gifts and offerings blind the eyes of the wise. Therefore, being solicitous to put an end to such shameful gain, we have decreed to provide from our pious treasury salaries for the most illustrious quaestor, for the registrars, and for the

chief officials employed in administering justice, to the intent that they may receive nothing from any person whomsoever he be, who may be tried before them, in order that what is said by the prophet may not be fulfilled in us, 'He sold justice for silver,' [Isaiah 5:23] and that we may not incur the wrath of God as transgressors of His commandments."

6. Examples include the Lex Salica of the Frankish King Clovis (about A.D. 511), the laws of the Anglo-Saxon King Ethelbert (about A.D. 600), and the *Russkaia Pravda* of the Kievan Prince Yaroslav (about A.D. 1030).

7. The Peace of God (*pax Dei,* also called *pax ecclesiae,* Peace of the Church), which originated at synods in France in 990, also forbade acts of private warfare against ecclesiastical property. Enforcement was weak, being vested in the bishop or count on whose lands violations occurred. The Truce of God (*treuga Dei*) originated at a synod of 1027. It was more successful, especially in the twelfth century when fighting was –in principle–outlawed during nearly three-fourths of the year.

8. The view that the Great Reform championed by Pope Gregory VII was the first of the Great Revolutions of European history was pioneered by Eugen Rosenstock-Huessy in *Die Europaeischen Revolutionen* (Jena, 1931). See also Eugen Rosenstock-Huessy, *Out of Revolution: The Autobiography of Western Man* (New York, 1938), and *The Driving Power of Western Civilization: The Christian Revolution of the Middle Ages* (Boston, 1949). Although Gregory is still viewed as a traditionalist and even a reactionary by a few historians, virtually none now deny that it was in his time that the Roman Catholic Church took its modern form as a legal institution. Cf. Schafer Williams, ed., *The Gregorian Epoch: Reformation, Revolution, Reaction?* (Boston, 1964); Brian Tierney, *The Crisis of Church & State 1050-1300* (Englewood Cliffs, N.J., 1964). With the current reform movement of the church initiated under Pope John XXIII, an increasing number of Roman Catholic advocates of radical change (such as Hans Küng of Germany, Leslie Dewart and Gregory

157

Baum of Canada, and others) have referred to Pope Gregory VII as the initiator of a new era in church history, one which they see as now coming to an end. Cf. Küng, *The Church* (New York, 1967), pp. 10, 384, 445, where it is stated that the view of the church as imposing authority "from above" originated with Gregory VII, and that at that time the clergy (*spirituales*) were formed into a legal body, separate from the laity (*carnales*). The church, Küng states, after the Gregorian reforms, was "organized strictly along juridical lines and by a monarchical universal episcopate."

An illuminating essay by Yves Congar, O.P., entitled "The Historical Development of Authority in the Church: Points for Christian Reflection," in John M. Todd, ed., *Problems of Authority: An Anglo-French Symposium* (London and Baltimore, 1962), pp. 119-55, states that "the reform begun by St. Leo IX (1049-54) and continued with such vigour by St. Gregory VII represents a decisive turning point from the point of view of ecclesiastical doctrines in general and of the notion of authority in particular." Congar points out that the search for legal texts to support Gregory's position marked the beginning of the science of canon law, and that the mystique of Gregory's program lay in its translation of absolute justice, or divine law, into a new system of church law, at the heart of which was the legal authority of the pope. "One is actually obeying God when one obeys his representative" (p. 139). The word church came to indicate "not so much the body of the faithful as the system, the apparatus" (p. 140). From the late eleventh century onward, Congar states, ecclesiastical authority, and especially the supreme authority of the pope, came to be stated in legal terms borrowed from the secular vocabulary. It was then, for example, that the term Papal Curia was first used—that is, it was then that the papal household was first conceived as a law court, with authority to review automatically the judgments handed down in all bishops' courts.

9. The text of Gregory VII's *Dictatus papae* (Dictates of the Pope) of 1075 may be found in Ernest F. Henderson, *Select Historical Documents of the Middle Ages* (New York,

1968), pp. 366-67, and in Frederic A. Ogg, *A Source Book of Medieval History* (New York, 1972), pp. 262-64. It reflected papal claims of supremacy over both the ecclesiastical and the secular realms. Some of the claims with respect to the secular realm had to be abandoned, but papal autocracy within the church has survived to this day. Among the most radical provisions of the *Dictatus* were the following:

"That the Roman bishop alone . . . has the power to depose bishops and reinstate them. . . . That he has the power to despose emperors. . . . That he may, if necessity require, transfer bishops from one see to another. . . . That he has power to ordain a clerk of any church he may wish. . . . That he can be judged by no man. . . . That no one shall dare to condemn a person who appeals to the apostolic see. . . . That to the latter should be referred the more important cases of every church. . . . That the Roman Church has never erred, nor ever, by the testimony of Scripture, shall err, to all eternity. . . . That no one can be considered Catholic who does not agree with the Roman Church. . . . That he [the pope] has the power to absolve the subjects of unjust rulers from their oath of fidelity."

10. A considerable discussion has resolved around the proposal to revise the Code of Canon Law, which in 1917 replaced the Decretals of Pope Gregory IX. The Second Vatican Council proposed that the code be thoroughly revised, and a commission has been constituted to prepare such a revision. The discussion of its revision has included arguments to the effect that law should be wholly eliminated from the life of the church. Cf. note 1, chapter III.

11. The passage, falsely attributed to St. Augustine, grows out of the penitentials of the tenth and eleventh centuries, which were the chief precursors of the modern system of canon law that was founded in the twelfth century by Gratian. It reads as follows: "For one who judges another . . . condemns himself. Let him therefore know himself and purge himself of what he sees offends others. *Let him who is without sin cast the first stone at her. (John, viii, 7)* . . . For no one

was without sin in that it is understood that all have been guilty of crime. For venial sins will always be remitted [only] by holy rites. If therefore the sin was one of these, it was criminal. . . . Let the spiritual judge beware, in order thereby not to commit the crime of injustice, that he not fail to fortify himself with knowledge. It is fitting that he should know how to recognize what he is to judge. For the judicial power is based on the assumption that he discerns what he is to judge. Therefore the diligent inquisitor, the subtle investigator, wisely and almost cunningly interrogates the sinner about that which the sinner perhaps does not know, or because of shame will wish to hide. . . . We write this to you, devotee of truth and lover of certainty, concerning true penitence, separating the true from the false. . . ." "De Vera et Falsa Poenitentia" c. XX. Migne, *Patrologia Latina,* XL (1129-30 [pseudo-Augustinian, *circa* 1050]).

This passage, which was incorporated by Gratian into his *Concordance of Discordant Canons,* expresses an idea which was unknown to the classical Roman law as well as to the previous law of the Church. It marks the transition from liturgical and sacramental thinking to a science of jurisprudence. Cf. Rudolph Sohm, *Das altkatholische Kirchenrecht und das Dekret Gratians* (Leipzig, 1918).

12. Rudolf Sohm, *Weltliches und geistliches Recht* (Munich and Leipzig, 1914), p. 69.

13. Cf. Gerrard Winstanley, *Platform of the Law of Freedom:* "The spirit of the whole creation was about the reformation of the world." Quoted in Rosenstock-Huessy, *Out of Revolution* p. 291. Cf. Thomas Case, sermon preached before the House of Commons in 1641: "Reformation must be universal. Reform all places, all persons and callings; reform the benches of judgment, the inferior magistrates. . . . Reform the universities, reform the cities, reform the countries, reform inferior schools of learning, reform the Sabbath, reform the ordinances, the worship of God. Every plant which my heavenly father hath not planted shall be rooted up." Quoted in Michael Walzer, *The Revolution of the Saints: A Study*

in the Origins of Radical Politics (Cambridge, Mass., 1965), pp. 10-11. The sixteenth-century Reformation was conceived as a reformation of the church; a century later the Puritans were seeking, in Milton's words, "the reforming of reformation itself," which meant, as Walzer shows, radical political activity, that is, political progress as a religious goal (p. 12).

14. Cf. A. D. Lindsay, *The Modern Democratic State* (New York, 1962), pp. 117-18; David Little, *Religion, Order, and Law: A Study in Pre-Revolutionary England* (New York, 1969), p. 230.

15. Each of the men named was charged with civil disobedience. Each defended himself on the basis of a higher law of conscience as well as on grounds of fundamental legal principles derived from medieval English law (e.g., Magna Carta). The trials of Penn and Hampden are reported in 6 *State Trials* 951 (1670) and 3 *State Trials* 1 (1627) (the Five Knights' Case). An extract of the trial of Udall, together with background information, may be found in Daniel Neal, *The History of the Puritans* (Newburyport, Mass., 1816), pp. 492-501. The trial of Lilburne is discussed in Joseph Frank, *The Levellers: A History of the Writings of Three 17th Century Social Democrats: John Lilburne, Richard Overton, and William Walwyn* (Cambridge, 1965), pp. 16-18.

16. This point is usually overlooked; instead, the theory of social contract is generally traced to seventeenth-century philosophers such as John Locke and Thomas Hobbes. But a century earlier, Calvin had asked the entire people of Geneva to accept the confession of faith and to take an oath to obey the Ten Commandments, as well as to swear loyalty to the city. People were summoned in groups by the police to participate in the covenant. Cf. J. T. McNeill, *The History and Character of Calvinism* (New York, 1957), p. 142.

17. Cf. Roscoe Pound, *Jurisprudence*, III (St. Paul, Minn., 1959), pp. 8-15.

18. The Moral Code of the Builder of Communism is part of the Program of the Communist Party of the Soviet Union adopted by the twenty-second Party Congress in 1961. It may

161

be found in Dan N. Jacobs, ed., *The New Communist Manifesto and Related Documents* (3rd rev. ed.; New York, 1965), p. 35.

19. See *The Laws and Liberties of Massachusetts* (Cambridge, Mass., 1929).

20. See Moltmann, *Religion, Revolution and the Future*, trans. Douglas Meeks (New York, 1969), pp. 113-17. Cf. Thomas Luckmann, *The Invisible Religion* (New York, 1967).

21. The phrase "religionless Christianity" is that of the German theologian Dietrich Bonhoeffer, who in his letters from a Nazi prison developed the idea that in contemporary twentieth-century society institutional religious forms and conventional religious doctrines are no longer needed and are, indeed, an obstacle to a Christian life. Here, however, we use the phrase in a somewhat different sense—to refer to the weakening of the social and historical dimensions of Christianity and its reduction to a private faith.

Chapter III

1. A radical distinction between law and love, in the terms stated in the text, may be found in Emil Brunner, *Justice and the Social Order* (New York, 1945), pp. 21 ff. Reinhold Niebuhr criticized Brunner for believing that "Christian love reveals itself . . . only in uniquely personal and intimate relations." "Brunner is in great error," he writes, "when he interprets an act of personal kindness as more 'Christian' than a statesmanlike scheme in the interest of justice. . . . The effort to confine *Agape* to the love of personal relations and to place all the structures and artifices of justice outside that realm makes Christian love irrelevant to the problems of man's common life." Reinhold Niebuhr, "Love and Law in Protestantism and Catholicism," *Journal of Religious Thought* IX (1952), 95-111. Niebuhr stated that "the distinction between law and love is less absolute and more dialectical than conceived in either Catholic or Reformation thought." He saw that the root of the error is not only in a sentimentalization of love but also in a mechanization of law—or, as he put it, "a

Stoic-Aristotelian rationalism which assumes fixed historical structures and norms which do not in fact exist." Unfortunately, Niebuhr himself was sometimes guilty of making the same error which he rightly attributes to Brunner; cf. his famous *Moral Man and Immoral Society* (New York, 1932).

St. Augustine's famous dictum is misinterpreted by those who would find support in it for a sharp contrast between "abstract" ethical or legal norms and "concrete" acts of love. St. Augustine contended that love for God is the primary virtue from which other virtues, including the virtue of justice, flow—so that one who truly loves God will naturally wish to act according to the norms which God prescribes. There is a lucid discussion of this in Edward LeRoy Long, Jr., *A Survey of Christian Ethics* (New York, 1967), pp. 129-31.

Among contemporary Roman Catholic scholars, John L. McKenzie, in *The Power and the Wisdom: An Interpretation of the New Testament* (Milwaukee, 1965), takes the view that "Christian freedom annuls law" (p. 207). See also Robert Adolfs, *The Church is Different* (New York, 1966), in which the author attacks legalism in the Roman Catholic Church, stating that "in the Christian ethic one thing and one thing only is prescribed—namely love—and the only intrinsic evil is lack of love" (p. 92). This tendency of current Roman Catholic thought has been criticized by Jean Lacroix, who states: "The great danger of our time, especially for Christians, is that of a disincarnated supernaturalism which is ready to sacrifice power, which misunderstands the role of law and imagines that all problems can be resolved by the witness of love." Quoted in Frederick J. Crosson, "Liberty and Authority," in James E. Biechler, ed., *Law for Liberty: The Role of Law in the Church Today* (Baltimore, 1967), p. 155. Cf. note 2 following.

2. The first of the two "love commandments" is found in Deuteronomy 6:5; the second is found in Leviticus 19:18; they are brought together in Matthew 23:34-40.

There is a widespread misconception that Judaism teaches that God is primarily a God of justice, while Christianity

teaches that he is a God of love. This misconception is refuted by almost all leading Christian and Jewish theologians. One of the more dramatic Jewish refutations is the rabbinical explanation of the fact that in the Bible there are two names for God: Adonai (Jehovah) and Elohim. It is said that Adonai is used when God is spoken of as being in close relationship with men and nations, while Elohim denotes God as creator and moral governor of the universe. Adonai stresses the loving-kindness and mercy of God, while Elohim emphasizes justice and rulership. The Midrash says that God, in creating the world, debated with himself whether he should create it by mercy or by justice. "If I create the world by mercy alone," he said to himself, "sin will abound. If I create it by justice alone, how can the world endure? Therefore," he concluded, "I will create it by both." And so in the first chapter of Genesis, when the story is told of how God created the world as a whole, the name Elohim—justice—is used, while in the second chapter of Genesis, when the story of man is told, "Adonai" (Jehovah) is used together with "Elohim." I am indebted to Rabbi Edward Zerin for calling my attention to this commentary, which may be found in J. H. Hertz, ed., *Chumash, The Soucino Edition of the Pentateuch and Haftorahs* (2nd ed., William Clowes and Sons, Ltd., London, n.d.), pp. 6-7.

3. See Joseph Fletcher, *Situation Ethics* (Philadelphia, 1966); Paul L. Lehmann, *Ethics in a Christian Context* (New York, 1963). Cf. Long, *A Survey of Christian Ethics*, pp. 157 ff; L. Harold DeWolf, *Responsible Freedom: Guidelines to Christian Action* (New York, 1971), pp. 28-30, 32-36, and especially 107-10 (where "love in the high New Testament sense" is defined as the "active quest for koinonia," a "deeply communal word," which gives rise to the church as an "organic community." Dr. DeWolf writes: "The idea of a single individual . . . loving other individuals while all remain 'separate but equal' in that individuality never appears" in the Old or New Testament.) Since love is communal it cannot operate without regular procedures and rules generated

by such procedures. Cf. Walter G. Muelder, *Foundations of the Responsible Society* (New York, 1959).

4. John T. Noonan, Jr. in the Preface to his book *Power to Dissolve: Lawyers and Marriages in the Courts of the Roman Curia* (Cambridge, Mass., 1972) pp. xii-xiii, admirably summarizes the problem of the compatibility of law and love. "In almost any contemporary system," he writes, "the compatibility of law with love is an issue; in a Christian system, it is crucial. According to evangelical authority, to love God with heart, mind, and soul, and to love one's neighbor as oneself are fundamental; the disciples of Jesus will be recognized by loving each other as He loved them. These principles, difficult of realization in any event, are particularly difficult for a legal system to incorporate. They are not realized if a system leads its responsible officials to think of the human beings in the process only in abstract aspects of their persons; or if concentration of attention on the machinery of procedure leads to forgetfulness of the system's subordination to these principles. If such effects appear to be inevitable in any system of law, so that men whose business it is to apply law to other men can never love them or be loved by them, no legal system is compatible with Christian principles. If, however, men are able to accept law as necessary for the creation of a community, pursuit of the communal purposes may bridge the unbridgeable gap between the general norm and the individual person. Realization of the principles of love will then depend on how consciously the common purposes are held, how effectively they are communicated, how faithfully they guide action."

5. Long, *A Survey of Christian Ethics*, pp. 188-89. The context of the quotation is Luther's discussion of the difference between individual and collective morality. He states that a Christian prince, to restrain sin, might be required to go to war, although for an individual Christian, acting as an invidual, it would be wrong to go to war. Thus secular law, for Luther, was a secondary matter, a matter of political necessity, whose purpose—from a Christian standpoint—was to

restrain sin; but the primary matter—justification—was the
result of individual faith.

6. *Ibid.*, p. 132. Luther "made categorical denials that the
doctrine of justification by faith can be used as an excuse
for release from ethical obligation." Long quotes Luther's
statement that "as faith makes a man a believer and righteous,
so faith also does good works" (p. 133).

7. Cf. *ibid.*, pp. 308, 309.

8. Cf. Harvey Cox, *The Secular City* (New York, 1965).

9. There is a considerable Protestant literature on "the uses
of the law." Although there are some differences between
Lutheran and Calvinist views on the subject (*see* Long, *A
Survey of Christian Ethics*, pp. 82 ff.), in general both
attribute to the law (including not only the moral law but
also its counterpart in the civil law of the state) three functions: (1) the function of deterring recalcitrant people from
misconduct by threat of penalties, (2) the function of making
people conscious of their obligations and hence repentant
of their sins, and (3) the function of guiding faithful people
in the paths of virtuous living. See the Lutheran Formula
of Concord, quoted in Alec R. Vidler, *Christ's Strange Work*
(London, 1944), pp. 21-22.

Of the third function, Calvin wrote: "The third use of the
law, which is the principal one, and which is more nearly connected with the proper end of it, relates to the faithful, in
whose hearts the Spirit of God already lives and reigns. For
although the law is inscribed and engraven on their hearts by
the finger of God—that is, although they are so excited and
animated by the direction of the Spirit, that they desire to
obey God—yet they derive a twofold advantage from the law.
For they find it an excellent instrument to give them, from
day to day, a better and more certain understanding of the
Divine will to which they aspire and to confirm them in the
knowledge of it. As, though a servant be already influenced by
the strongest desire of gaining the approbation of his master,
yet it is necessary for him carefully to inquire and observe the
orders of his master, in order to conform to them. Nor let

anyone of us exempt himself from this necessity; for no man has already acquired so much wisdom, that he could not by the daily instruction of the law make new advances into a purer knowledge of the Divine will. In the next place, as we need not only instruction, but also exhortation, the servant of God will derive this further advantage from the law; by frequent meditation on it he will be excited to obedience, he will be confirmed in it, and restrained from the slippery path of transgression." John Calvin, *Institutes of the Christian Religion,* trans. John Allen, Bk. II, Ch. VII, par. xii.

A fine essay applying the Lutheran Formula to contemporary problems is Wilber G. Katz's "Moral Theology and the Criminal Law," *Anglican Theological Review,* July, 1956.

10. See preceding note.

11. " 'Religion is a private matter.' With this shibboleth, modern society has freed itself from any public influence of the various Christian confessions. But inherent in this movement is the simultaneous relegation of religion to a new function. Religion now becomes the cult of the private, *cultus privatus.* Religion is now understood as a matter of inwardness and feeling, a special attribute of the 'personal.' . . . Religion and faith must concern themselves with the lonely, unsettled soul, with the inner existence of modern man, an existence which has been called into question by the modern world. . . . It can no longer be demonstrated that God is the origin and goal of the world and of human society within the world process, but it can be demonstrated that God is the transcendental ground of existence, of the capacity to act personally and according to conscience. It is no longer possible to create room for God in the sphere of worldly knowledge and activity. [This] leaves Christianity with nothing to say to the world other than what this world wants to hear." Jürgen Moltmann, *Religion, Revolution and the Future,* pp. 113, 117.

12. C. H. Dodd, *The Interpretation of the Fourth Gospel,* (Cambridge, 1970), pp. 82 ff.

13. Cf. Theodore Roszak, *The Making of a Counter-Culture* (New York, 1969).

14. Charles Reich, *The Greening of America* (New York, 1970).
15. That the counterculture is itself a derivation from Christianity is ignored in Roszak's otherwise excellent book as well as in Reich's book and in most other literature on the subject. However, William Braden, in *The Age of Aquarius* (New York, 1970), finds some connections between the "cultural revolution" and certain trends in theology (the theology of hope); and in 1970 and 1971 those connections became more prominent as many communes emerged whose orientation was avowedly Christian (e.g., "Jesus Freaks").
16. Ezekiel 33:11. Cf. Jacques Ellul, *The Theological Foundation of Law* (New York, 1969), p. 39. Ellul sharply distinguishes divine justice from human justice and attacks natural-law theory as "nothing more than the transportation into heaven of relative and terrestrial justice. . . . Nowhere in biblical revelation is there any mention made of [natural law]" (p. 64). Since man is by nature evil and unjust, Ellul states, he is incapable of creating something which is just (p. 71). He further contends that "the state has no business punishing moral evil and sin" (p. 124). Yet near the end of the book, Ellul makes a complete about-face, arguing that human law, despite its imperfection, does "remind us" of God's righteousness and further, that human law "cannot be separated from compassion," and that it has a universality which transcends national differences (pp. 115-21).
17. "I will set my law within them and write it on their hearts; I will become their God and they shall become my people" (Jer. 31:33-34).
18. The words are those of Justice Oliver Wendell Holmes in a letter to Harold Laski: "If I were having a philosophical talk with a man I was going to have hanged (or electrocuted) I should say, I don't doubt that your act was inevitable for you but to make it more avoidable by others we propose to sacrifice you to the common good. You may regard yourself as a soldier dying for your country if you like. But the law must keep its promises." In an illuminating commentary, Wilber G. Katz writes:

"This quotation may strike the reader with something of a shock. And it may seem more shocking that theologians in the classical Protestant tradition are just as unapologetic about treating criminals as instruments for social purposes. . . . Moralists have often attacked this view as to the purpose of punishment. Kant insisted that it is utterly immoral for society to treat a man as a means to be used for its purposes. The only morally defensible basis of punishment, according to Kant, is that of retribution for acts freely chosen. But on this point the Judeo-Christian tradition—with its 'realistic' insights as to human nature paralleling those of dynamic psychology—is closer to modern positivism than to ethical idealism. Theologians in this tradition do not base criminal responsibility upon a relatively untrammeled freedom of choice. Their position is therefore not shaken by the findings of psychological and social science as to the great extent to which human conduct is determined. . . . As Paul Tillich puts it, 'Love, in order to exercise its proper work, namely charity and forgiveness, must provide for a place on which this can be done, through its strange work of judging and punishing.'" Wilber G. Katz, "Moral Theology and the Criminal Law," pp. 5-6. The quotation from Tillich is from his *Love, Power, and Justice* (New York, 1954), p. 49. The phrase "strange work" used by Tillich is from the Lutheran Formula of Concord, in which the law is characterized as "Christ's strange work." See also note 9 of this chapter.

Chapter IV

1. The preceding interpretation of the significance of the Legend of the Grand Inquisitor, though unconventional, is supported generally by modern scholarship concerning the "polyphonic" character of Dostoevsky's writings. See M. Bakhtin, *Problemy poetiki Dostoevskogo* (2nd ed., Moscow, 1963), especially pp. 332 ff. (French edition, *Problèmes de la poétique de Dotoïevski* [Lausanne, 1970], pp. 290 ff.) The conflict between Ivan and Alyosha is also a conflict within each, which is resolved only by the book as a whole. Indeed, it is not

169

fully resolved even then, for *The Brothers Karamazov* (like *Moby Dick*) is a kind of "Old Testament" in which there is a latent "New Testament," that Dostoevsky, however, (like Melville) was unable to write.

2. See *The Brothers Karamazov* (Garnett trans., New York, 1929), pp. 70 ff.

3. Cf. chapter I, note 24.

4. Jeremy Bentham has perhaps given the principle of dualism its most systematic rationalization and application. He believed that to achieve certainty it was necessary to classify all knowledge into mutually exclusive "bifurcations." "Thus, if we have a division of an aggregate into three," he wrote, "we cannot give such a nomenclature to these three elements as will show that they exhaust the aggregate. If we say the law is divided into penal and non-penal, we feel certain, in the very form of the statement, that we include every sort of law under one or other of these designations." And again: "It is only by the expression of a difference as between two, that thought and language enable us to say whether the elements of the things divided are exhausted in the condividends. We can only compare two things together—we cannot compare three or more at a time. In common language we do speak of comparing together more things than two, but the operation by which we accomplish this end is compound, consisting of deductions drawn from a series of comparisons, each relating to only two things at a time." See C. K. Ogden, *Bentham's Theory of Fictions* (London, 1932), pp. cxxvi, cxxv. According to Bentham, either a thing is so or it is not so; either it is physical or it is psychical; either a proposition is clear or it is ambiguous; either a law is penal or it is not penal; either an entity is real or it is fictitious, etc. Admittedly, this "bifurcate system," as he called it, may have some utility as a method of exposition so long as the expositor and his reader or listener attach the same meanings to the "condividends"; but Bentham used it also as a method of knowing reality and of exhausting its nature. In reality, however, opposites combine. Today, at least, we can no longer

accept truth simply in "either-or" terms; again and again it presents itself to us as "both-and."

5. See Leslie Dewart, *The Future of Belief: Theism in a World Come of Age* (New York, 1966), pp. 152-70; Dewart, *The Foundations of Belief* (New York, 1969), pp. 347 ff. Dewart has attacked the elements of Hellenism in Roman Catholic thought, and especially the Platonic assumption that language (and hence thought) merely reflects the structure of reality. Through language and thought, he writes, we do not merely reflect reality or observe it; rather it is their function "actively to *situate* man in the reality of the world" (p. 416). Cf. p. 225.

6. The concept of legal decision-making as a "policy science" has been associated in the United States in recent decades primarily with the writings of Professors Harold Lasswell and Myres McDougal of the Yale University Law School. These writers share with the so-called Legal Realists the view that rules of law announced by judges as the reasons for their decisions are in fact only rationalizations of results reached on other (extralegal) grounds. They attempt to go beyond Legal Realism, however, by propounding a set of economic, political, sociological, psychological, and other "values" by which the judges' preferences ought to be guided. Cf. McDougal, "The Law School of the Future: From Legal Realism to Policy Science in the World Community," *Yale Law Journal* LVI (1947), 1345. The popularity of the "policy science" school of legal thought has coincided with a marked increase of what is often called "judicial activism"— including expansion of jurisdiction, overruling of precedents, and reasoning in terms of social consequences—on the part of many courts, including especially the Supreme Court of the United States. An important attack upon judicial usurpation and arbitrariness was made by Professor Herbert Wechsler of the Columbia University Law School in his 1959 Holmes Lectures at Harvard; see Wechsler, "Toward Neutral Principles of Constitutional Law," *Harvard Law Review* LXXIII (1959), 1. The debate between advocates of "policy" and

advocates of "neutral principles" continued to rage in legal literature during the 1960s and into the 1970s, just as the conflict between "judicial activism" and "judicial self-restraint" continued to divide the judiciary.

7. Zechariah Chafee, Jr., "Do Judges Make or Discover Law?" *Proceedings of American Philosophical Society* 91 (1947), 405.

8. See chapter 1, note 13. Cf. Norman O. Brown, *Love's Body* (New York, 1968), pp. 201 ff. Elsewhere Brown writes: "The classical Western sense of time, Newtonian time, was a religion, which, like all religions, was taken by its adherents (both the physicists and the economists) to be absolute objective truth. Once again, we see that 'secular rationalism' is really a religion; the new relativist notion of time is really the disintegration of a religion." See *Life Against Death: The Psychoanalytical Meaning of History* (Middletown, Conn., 1959), p. 274.

9. Brown, *Love's Body*, pp. 219, 220.

10. Rosenstock-Huessy, *Out of Revolution: The Autobiography of Western Man.*

11. *The Christian Future* (New York, 1946), p. 70. "The anticipation of a Last Judgment looming over our own civilization is the best remedy against its inevitable downfall" (*Out of Revolution*, p. 561); cf. Eugen Rosenstock and Joseph Wittig, *Das Alter der Kirche*, I (Berlin, 1927), 84 ff.

12. Cf. Long, *A Survey of Christian Ethics*, p. 34.

13. See Page Smith, *As a City Upon a Hill* (New York, 1968). This important book, which is subtitled *The Town in American History*, could well have been subtitled "The Commune in American History." It is about the concept of the covenanted community as it manifested itself in the spread of small "colonized" towns throughout America from the early seventeenth century until the end of the nineteenth century. The utopian communes of the Shakers, Owenites, Amish, Fourierists, and others are seen by Professor Smith as aberrant forms of the more typical new towns settled by people fleeing from the strife, corruption, and greed which had corroded the

old covenant. Written largely before the revival of communal movements in the late 1960s (the Introduction is dated February 1966), Professor Smith's book does comment, in a footnote at the very end, upon the connection between the decline of "organic" communities and the problem of alienation. This leads to the development of "pseudo-communities" among groups of individuals who share some critical problem of social adjustment or personal malaise. In his conclusion Professor Smith writes of the American town: "The builders of the town were obsessed by the dream of 'the good community' where greed, factionalism, poverty, and inequality were to be banished. Their values were oriented toward the community rather than toward the individual. The dreams failed of fulfillment and there was much bitterness in that failure. Making it more bitter was the fact that the town from having been the microcosm, the measure, of the larger society, the asserter of its values and the shaper of its ideals, came to lust after city ways and manners, after the city's success. The city's version of the Protestant ethic at last came to be universally accepted, and was, as a final irony, attributed to the small town" (p. 307).

14. In *Commitment and Community: Communes, and Utopias in Sociological Perspective* (Cambridge, Mass., 1972), Rosabeth Moss Kanter discusses the adverse effects of the temporary character of communal life. She asks "whether communes are indeed a solution to the alienation suffered by American society if they do not provide long-term relationships" (pp. 215-16). Also she states that "it is often demoralizing for a group—even the most 'hang loose,' 'do your own thing' group —to face a continual turnover by losing members or to contemplate dissolution" (p. 16). These observations seem to presuppose that it is the function of the commune to permanently replace the larger society of which it is a part. She comes closer to the point when she recognizes (p. 217) that "at the very least, certain [short-lived] communes, like encounter groups, may help to educate people in the possibilities for alternative modes of living and relating."

Postscript

1. "In all cultures and in all systems of thought . . . what is socially lawful and unlawful is related to what is morally right and wrong, and everywhere the moral law is based ultimately on religious sanctions." Christopher Dawson, *Religion and Culture* (New York, 1948), p. 155. Cf. Arthur L. Harding, ed., *Religion, Morality, and Law* (Dallas, 1956), in which the first chapter is entitled "Can There Be Morality Without Religion?" and the second chapter is entitled "Can There Be Law Without Morality?" However, to focus on morality as the principal link between law and religion is to exaggerate the role of general rules in both law and religion and to underestimate the role of ritual, tradition, authority, and universality (see chapter I.) The category of universality overlaps morality but places more stress on aspiration than on duty. In general, I oppose the effort to reduce either law or religion to morality—or to metaphysics. Both law and religion are social enterprises; each has its own symbolic language; each is valuable for its own sake—as a dimension of human experience.

D1321321